# AUTUMN GLEANINGS

OTHER PUBLICATIONS BY THE DURRELL
SCHOOL OF CORFU

*Lawrence Durrell: The Mindscape*
by Richard Pine, revised edition (2005)

*A Chronology of the Life and Times of Lawrence Durrell
Homme de Lettres*
by Brewster Chamberlin (2007)

*Nostos: Proceedings of the Durrell School
of Corfu, 1: 2002–2005*
edited by Richard Pine (2008)

*Judith: A Novel*
by Lawrence Durrell
edited by Richard Pine (2012)

# AUTUMN GLEANINGS

## CORFU MEMOIRS AND POEMS

by

# THEODORE STEPHANIDES

edited by
Richard Pine,
Lindsay Parker, James Gifford
and Anthony Hirst

The Durrell School of Corfu
in conjunction with
The International Lawrence Durrell Society
2011

DURRELL SCHOOL OF CORFU
11 FILELLINON
PO BOX 94
CORFU, GREECE 49-100
www.durrell-school-corfu.org

INTERNATIONAL LAWRENCE DURRELL SOCIETY
PINE BLUFF, AR, USA
www.lawrencedurrell.org

AUTUMN GLEANINGS
© Estate of Theodore Stephanides 2011

ISBN: 978-0-9549937-3-3

First published 2011
Reprinted with minor corrections 2012
Reprinted with further corrections 2015

Printed and bound in the Great Britain by
Lightning Source UK Ltd
Chapter House, Pitfield, Kiln Farm
Milton Keynes MK11 3LW

# Table of Contents

| | |
|---|---|
| Editor's Introduction | 9 |
| Theodore Stephanides: A Brief Biography | 12 |
| Select Bibliography | 19 |
| Corfu Memoirs | 23 |
|     First Meeting with Lawrence Durrell – Building of the House at Kalami (Top Floor) | 25 |
|     The 'Ionian Banquets' | 35 |
|     Lawrence Durrell and Nature | 40 |
|     Days at Palaeocastritsa | 47 |
|     At the Villa Anemoyanni | 55 |
|     Kalami Again | 57 |
|     Spyros the Chauffeur Drives Us to Palaeocastritsa | 62 |
|     The Palatiano Villa | 65 |
|     Lawrence Durrell and the Greek Shadow Play | 68 |
|     Paper Games, Corfu | 70 |
|     Some Victorian Relics | 73 |
|     In Athens – Early Days of World War II | 75 |
|     In Egypt after the Fall of Crete | 78 |
|     *From Stephanides' Correspondence* | 86 |
| Autumn Gleanings (poems) | 89 |
|     Aurora Borealis | 91 |
|     Distant Thunderstorm at Night | 91 |
|     Sunset | 92 |
|     The Universe | 92 |
|     Insomnia | 93 |
|     Question | 93 |
|     Ice Age | 94 |
|     Termite Cosmologist | 95 |
|     Five Quatrains: *Eclipse – Air waves – Homo superior – The goad – Skylark* | 96 |
|     Hail on a Tin Roof | 97 |
|     Christmas Aftermath | 97 |

[AUTUMN GLEANINGS (POEMS), CONTINUED]

| | |
|---|---:|
| Celestial Paradox | 98 |
| First Greeting | 99 |
| Golden Lyre | 99 |
| Miscalculation | 100 |
| London under Snow | 100 |
| London Plane (*Platanus acerifolia* Wildenow) | 101 |
| Five Quatrains: *Points of view — Verdict — Diatoms seen under the microscope — The lonely fir tree — Cloud-shadows* | 102 |
| Song of Oncoming Spring | 103 |
| Egocentrism | 104 |
| Pauper's Burial | 105 |
| Palinode (Song) | 105 |
| Two Seagulls (Oxford, March 1958) | 106 |
| Five Quatrains: *Impossible task — Death — Prayer — Atlantis — Magnets* | 107 |
| Dead Leaves | 108 |
| Oncoming Eld | 108 |
| Red Upas | 109 |
| Query | 109 |
| The Perfect Demagogue | 110 |
| Orator | 110 |
| Five Quatrains: *Corcyra — Nostalgia for the past — Cyprus 1974 . . . — After the blow-up — Dirge* | 111 |
| No Hero | 112 |
| Historian's Headache | 112 |
| My Fair-Haired Darling (*after Solomos*) | 113 |
| Epitaph to the Island of Psara (*after Solomos*) | 114 |
| Flowers | 114 |
| The Haunted Tarn | 115 |
| Roses (*after a Greek folk-song*) | 115 |
| Five Quatrains: *Predicament — The torch — Convivial love — Paradox — Love's tempest* | 116 |
| The Pyre (*after a Greek folk-song*) | 117 |
| Inquest | 117 |
| Tree of Remembrance | 118 |
| Exoneration | 118 |
| Song | 119 |
| Threnody | 119 |
| Delayed Journey | 132 |

[AUTUMN GLEANINGS (POEMS), CONTINUED]

| | |
|---|---|
| Five Quatrains: *Wasted arrow — Radiance — Entreaty — Reproach — Love's Icarus* | 121 |
| Ghostly Ballad | 122 |
| The Tale of Prue, the Prudent Vampire | 126 |
| The Tempest, *or the unfortunate influence of motoring on the muse* | 128 |
| Five Quatrains: *Sport up to date — "When soft voices die" — The hypochondriach's epitaph — Divergence — Remedy* | 130 |
| The Wreck of the Schooner *Hesperus* | 131 |
| Not So *Piano* | 133 |
| My Love Came Tripping, Tripping . . . | 133 |
| Eight Distichs: *Revolt — Distraction — Politician — Immoral tale — Relativity — Nature note — Verdict — Moth* | 134 |
| Complaint | 135 |
| Bad Currency | 135 |
| After Many Years | 136 |
| Ultimate Goal | 136 |
| 80th Birthday (21–I–1976) | 137 |
| Evening Doubts (1978) | 137 |
| Five Quatrains: *Epitaph to a politician — Poet's predicament — The modern poet — Endeavour — The Parthenon* | 138 |

Bishop's Move     139

# Editor's Introduction

In 2006 James Gifford, my colleague in the Durrell School of Corfu, was assisting Anne Walker in the distribution of the papers of her late husband, James A. Brigham (1941–2005), formerly professor of English at Okanagan University College in British Columbia, Canada. 'Jay' Brigham was my friend, a profound scholar of the work of Lawrence Durrell, who was responsible for the edition of Durrell's Collected Poems in 1980.[1] Among Jay's papers, James Gifford found the typescripts of a series of memoirs of Lawrence Durrell by his lifelong friend Theodore Stephanides (1896–1983). Jay had published an edited version of these memoirs in *Deus Loci*, the journal of the International Lawrence Durrell Society, which he co-edited with Ian MacNiven, but the typescript located by Gifford revealed that there was far more material than Jay had been able to include in *Deus Loci*, material which adds considerably to our knowledge of Lawrence and Nancy Durrell's years in Corfu. The previous publication in *Deus Loci*, which today is largely inaccessible to the general reader, was partial, due to restrictions of space. These memoirs are valuable first-hand evidence of Lawrence's time in Corfu and Egypt. In some details, they conflict with – or certainly overlap – the received narrative of the Durrells' life in Corfu, but they do in some respects confirm the recently published article by Peter Harrison, 'The Durrells and Corfu',[2] and indicate that Lawrence and Nancy by no means lived exclusively at the White House at Kalami: they seem to have migrated quite regularly between Kalami (Lawrence's main writing base), the cottages rented by Stephanides himself at Palaeocastritsa, and the various villas rented by Lawrence's and Gerald Durrell's

---

[1] L. Durrell, *Collected Poems 1931–1974*, ed. James A. Brigham (London: Faber and Faber, 1980). J. Brigham's correspondence with Theodore Stephanides is held at the University of Victoria, as are the typescripts of the memoirs published in the present volume.
[2] *The Corfiot*, no. 210, June 2008.

mother at Perama and Kontokali.

The typescripts of these memoirs have been transcribed by Lindsay Parker and annotated by Parker and myself and are published here, in full, for the first time. Also included is a 'squib', entitled 'Bishop's Move', which first appeared in a commemorative Stephanides issue of *Deus Loci* in 1983.

Almost simultaneously with Gifford's discovery of these memoirs, I quite serendipitously acquired a copy of Theodore Stephanides' poems 'Autumn Gleanings'. I had been browsing the internet in search of volumes by Stephanides to complete our collection in the library of the Durrell School of Corfu (DSC) and, for a very modest sum, I purchased 'Autumn Gleanings', a title of which (naturally, as I discovered) I had been unaware. My surprise was very pronounced when I received the item: it consisted of a card cover, into which had been stitched a typescript of poems, carefully arranged by the author, the significance of which had clearly escaped the attention of the bookseller. Its provenance is unknown.

Stephanides' daughter, Alexia, had been unaware of the existence of these late-life poems by her father, but graciously consented to their publication, together with the earlier memoirs. (Annotations to the poems are my own.) From the evidence of the typescript, at least three copies of the poems exist, since the copy now in the DSC consists of some pages of top copy, some of carbon copy and some of sub-carbon copy. I subsequently discovered that another copy is in the custody of the Greek critic Marios Byron Raizis, who was asked by Stephanides to find a publisher for them (he was unsuccessful in this regard) and who has described his discussions with Stephanides in his essay 'Lawrence Durrell and the Greek Poets', which also lists six other unpublished works by Stephanides.[3]

---

[3] Marios Byron Raizis, 'Lawrence Durrell and the Greek Poets: A Contribution to Cultural History' in Anna Lillios (ed.), *Lawrence Durrell and the Greek World* (Selinsgrove: Susquehanna University Press; and London: Associated University Presses, 2004).

By this fortunate coincidence it has been possible for the DSC, by publishing the memoirs and the poems in one volume under the collective title *Autumn Gleanings*, to pay a double tribute to the man who not only guided Gerald Durrell into the career in which he became famous worldwide as a naturalist and zoologist, but also collaborated with Lawrence Durrell on the material for the latter's *Prospero's Cell* and became an important translator of Greek poetry, especially that of Kostes Palamas (in collaboration with George Katsimbalis), and the seventeenth-century Cretan verse romance, *Erotocritos* by Vitzentzos Kornaros. After the death of Katsimbalis, Theodore, as his daughter recalls, 'felt bereft and alone' in the absence of his collaborator. It was in these circumstances that he embarked, single-handed, on the translation of *Erotocritos*.

This volume is dedicated, with affection, to Theodore Stephanides' daughter, Alexia Stephanides-Mercouri and to her husband, the theatre historian and exhibition curator Spiros Mercouris. Its publication coincides with the unveiling of a plaque commemorating Theodore Stephanides, poet, translator and scientist, on the site of his laboratory and consulting rooms in Odos Mantzarou.

ACKNOWLEDGEMENTS

This publication would not have been possible without the advice, support and encouragement of Anne Walker, James Gifford, Lindsay Parker, Alexina Ashcroft (Administrative Director of the DSC), Alexia Stephanides-Mercouri, Dr Spiros Giourgas, Anthony Hirst, Corinne Alexandre-Garner, Barbara Papastavrou-Koroniotakis, and the Special Collections of the University of Victoria, Canada.

Richard Pine
Durrell School of Corfu
Greek Independence Day
25 March 2010

# THEODORE STEPHANIDES: A BRIEF BIOGRAPHY[4]

Theodore Philip Stephanides was born on 21 January 1896 in Bombay, India, where his father, a native of Thessaly, worked for the international company of Ralli Brothers, whose family was originally from Chios.[5] Known as 'Philip le beau', he married the boss's daughter, Caterina Ralli, who had been born and educated in London. As a result, Theodore had both English and Greek as his first languages. When his father retired in 1907 they moved to Corfu, where the Rallis family had an estate. Corfu was to be the venue for Theodore's remarkable meetings with the brothers Lawrence and Gerald Durrell in the 1930s, providing the basis for the memoirs printed here *verbatim* for the first time.

During the First World War, which began when he was eighteen years of age, Theodore served as a gunner in the Greek army on the Macedonian front, following which he saw service in the disastrous Anatolian campaign of 1919–22. His wartime experiences were not very successful, but the accounts of his service are typical not only of his own wry humour in reporting them, but also of the way in which his acquaintances relished the bizarre situations in which he found himself. Alan Thomas, who himself became a close friend of Stephanides, relates that the trainee gunner, given the task of firing a test-shot, 'worked out the bearings over and over again with his habitual scientific accuracy. The great moment came, the gun fired, and the

---

[4] It is to be hoped that a more extensive biography can be written, perhaps incorporating further excerpts from Stephanides' still unpublished plays, poems and correspondence, a significant amount of the last, with Lawrence Durrell, being now in the public domain.

[5] The Indian part of the company, established in 1854, dealt in jute, rice, saltpetre and spices. It closed after the 1929 international financial crash but re-opened after Indian independence. Today, by coincidence, it is part of the Tata conglomerate, founded in 1868, one of India's largest industrial concerns; Lawrence Durrell's father was responsible for building the Tata company's iron and steel works in the 1900s.

projectile landed upon a tent, belonging to the medical corps, in which a surgical operation was in progress… "I am probably the only doctor", Theodore is accustomed to recall with a smile, "who has dropped a shell into an operating theatre!".'[6] His experience in the Anatolian campaign was no less undistinguished. His commanding officer gave him the task of leading the entry into Smyrna on a white horse. 'I had learned to ride, but I would not consider myself an expert horseman… As I was riding at the head of the column, an old woman darted out of a side street and started to hurl eau-de-Cologne about. The horse… became most upset about it and was acting more like a circus horse than a charger. I only managed to stay on because my feet had become wedged in the stirrups. The column had to break ranks to try to calm him down, but he was so upset that eventually the commander decided that it would be unwise to let him take part in the rest of the triumphal entry. So while the column marched through the main streets with bands playing and people cheering and so forth, I was forced to slink through the back streets on my white horse, both of us, to add insult to injury, by now smelling very strongly of eau-de-Cologne… I have never really *enjoyed* horse-riding since then.'[7]

In 1922 Theodore went to Paris to study medicine and to specialise in radiology, one of his professors being Marie Curie. In Paris, Theodore also discovered and developed his passion for astronomy, which remained his chief interest right up to his death (and which is reflected in many of the poems published here). He was encouraged in this pursuit by one of the leading French astronomers, Camille Flammarion (1842–1925)[8] who wanted to make Theodore his chief pupil and heir. The 1930s saw him practising in Corfu as a radiologist, and marrying

---

[6] In Lawrence Durrell, *Spirit of Place*, ed. Alan Thomas (London: Faber and Faber, 1969), p. 57.
[7] In Gerald Durrell, *My Family and Other Animals*, in *The Corfu Trilogy* (London: Penguin Books, 2006), pp. 111–12.
[8] Brother of Ernest Flammarion, founder of the Flammarion publishing house.

Mary Alexander (a granddaughter of a former British consul in Corfu), with whom he had one daughter, Alexia. These years also saw him developing his skills as a freshwater biologist, and in the years 1938–39 he conducted significant work for the anti-malaria campaign in Salonica and Cyprus, funded by the Rockefeller Foundation. At this stage he had already written his scientific *magnum opus*, a treatise on the freshwater biology of Corfu, commissioned in 1936 by the Greek government, which was eventually published in 1948, and had been credited with the discovery of three microscopic water organisms, *Cytherois stephanidesi*, *Thermocyclops stephanidesi* and *Schizopera stephanidesi*. As is evident from his memoirs of Corfu, Stephanides was also an astronomer, and is the only person to have named after him not only three of nature's smallest water-creatures but also a crater on the moon ('Römer A' is unofficially named 'Stephanides crater').

During the Second World War, due to his dual Greek and British nationality, Theodore was a medical officer with the Royal Army Medical Corps in the African Western Desert, Sicily and Crete. In these years he renewed his acquaintance with Lawrence Durrell, who was working in Alexandria and Cairo; and his experiences in Crete led to the publication of his account of the campaign there, with a foreword by Durrell. His parents were killed during the German bombardment of Corfu, but his wife and Alexia had been taken to safety in England and, for some time, lived with the other members of the Durrell family who had returned from Corfu to Bournemouth at the outbreak of war.

At the end of the war, Theodore rejoined his family and, from 1945 until his retirement in 1961, worked as a radiologist at St Thomas's Hospital in the London borough of Lambeth. It was during this period that his remarkable flowering as a 'man of letters' occurred, with three volumes of poetry, several volumes of translation of the Greek poet Kostes Palamas (in collaboration with George Katsimbalis), a treatise on the microscope and other works, some of them still unpublished. He continued to write and undertake research, appearing with Gerald Durrell in the latter's BBC documentary on Corfu, *The Garden of the Gods* of 1967, and working on a proposed but unrealised collaboration with Lawrence Durrell on the history of the *Karaghiozis* shadow-puppet, which they had first encountered in Corfu in the 1930s. He died on 13 April 1983.

But these bare facts of his career hardly reflect Stephanides the man. If, for example, one were to compile a 'Collected Works of Theodore Stephanides', it would present a remarkably eclectic and wide-ranging series of *topoi*. Stephanides was a poet; he was a translator; he was a scientist; he was a traveller. And he wrote widely and deeply in all these epiphanies.

Although he began his work as a translator early in life with two volumes of Greek poetry in 1925 and 1926, together with his lifelong collaborator George Katsimbalis, his main contribution to the appearance in English of the poetry of Kostes Palamas was not to occur until after his retirement in 1961. Katsimbalis himself said that his own contribution was unnecessary, since Stephanides had sufficient command of both Greek and English, but Theodore seems to have felt a need for a second opinion from someone steeped in Greek literature, and his volumes, whether or not Katsimbalis contributed much to the translations, appeared under both their names.

Nevertheless, the published work, however varied it may be (as our bibliography indicates), gives only some of the flavour of the man who made such an impact on Lawrence Durrell and Gerald Durrell. Lawrence's *The Greek Islands*, and Gerald's *Birds, Beasts and Relatives* ('in gratitude for laughter and for learning') and *The Amateur Naturalist* were all dedicated to Theodore, as was Lawrence's as yet unpublished novella, 'The Magnetic Island': 'dedicated to Doctor Theodore Stephanides of the island of Corfu in memory of four years of a charmed friendship'.[9] Gerald's dedication of *The Amateur Naturalist* is even

---

[9] The typescript of 'The Magnetic Island' is at Southern Illinois University, Carbondale.

more explicit: 'This book is for Theo (Dr Theodore Stephanides) my mentor and friend, without whose guidance I would have achieved nothing'. For a very obvious but regrettable reason, Gerald is almost completely ignored in the memoirs. This, one assumes, is because Stephanides was trying to record his adult friendship with Lawrence, who was so clearly a writer-in-the-making, whereas Gerald was, at that time, little more than an impressionable child. Nevertheless, readers of *My Family and Other Animals*, in which Theodore is portrayed so warmly, affectionately and humorously, will regret that there is no mirror-image by Theodore of Gerald.

As Gerald recorded in his introduction to *Island Trails*, Theodore 'strolled into my life, tweed-suited, trilby-hatted, his walking stick with its tiny net on the end, his bag of test tubes and bottles slung on his hip, his beard twinkling in the sun; a sort of walking hirsute encyclopaedia... To me, just starting to explore and learn about the world I lived in, to have Theodore as guide, philosopher and friend was one of the most important things that have happened to me in my life.' Elsewhere, Gerald wrote of their first meeting 'He had a straight, well-shaped nose; a humorous mouth lurking in the ash-blond beard; straight, rather bushy eyebrows under which his eyes, keen but with a twinkle in them and laughter-wrinkles at the corners, surveyed the world.'[10] At the same time, Lawrence was recording a 'very Edwardian face – and perfect manners of Edwardian professor. Probably reincarnation of comic professor invented by Edward Lear during his stay in Corcyra. Tremendous shyness and diffidence. Incredibly erudite in everything concerning the island. Firm Venizelist,[11] and possessor of the driest and most fastidious style of exposition ever seen... Theodore is always being arrested as a foreign agent because of the golden beard, strong English accent in Greek, and mysterious array of vessels and swabs and tubes

---

[10] *Corfu Trilogy*, p. 75.
[11] Supporter of Eleftherios Venizelos, one of the major figures of Greek politics in the first half of the twentieth century.

dangling about his person.'[12] And when Henry Miller met him in 1939 he thought 'Theodore is the most learned man I have ever met, and a saint to boot.'[13]

Introducing Stephanides' 'Synoptic History' of Corfu, John Forte referred to him as 'an integral part and parcel of the island of Corfu and could in fact be described as a Corfiot institution'.[14] Although he had left Corfu at the outbreak of the Second World War, returning only infrequently, the island had been an inspiration to the young Stephanides, as it was in turn to the young Gerald Durrell (they were of very similar ages when they made their 'landfall' here), and this is clear in the many references to the island in Stephanides' poems, and, of course, explicit in his memoir of Lawrence Durrell at Kalami and Palaeocastritsa.

As the editor of this volume, I am amazed at my feeling that I actually *know* Theodore Stephanides – someone whom I never met. His zest for his work, his insight into, and pleasure in, the natural world, his humour, his deep sense of humanity, have brought him very close to me – merely a reader of his words. The same sense of attachment occurred to James Gifford and Lindsay Parker when reading through the memoirs published here. Behind his many volumes and articles in learned journals is the character who shyly appears within the pages of *The Corfu Trilogy* and perhaps one thinks one 'knows' him because Gerald brought him – his scholarship worn so lightly, his curiosity and passion for the world about him, his sense of humour – into such brilliant relief. The brief (one might almost say 'cameo') appearance in Gerald's television programme *The Garden of the Gods* serves to confirm both his eminence and his humanity, the latter quality shining through the poems published here. But what shines through Gerald's and Lawrence's remembrances of this astonishing man is his

---

[12] *Prospero's Cell* (London: Faber and Faber, 1945), p. 5.
[13] *The Colossus of Maroussi* (London: Secker and Warburg, 1942), p. 15.
[14] It is almost certain that, although this 'Synoptic History' was unpublished until 1963, it is the same text as that referred to by Lawrence Durrell in his *Prospero's Cell*.

high intelligence married to a phenomenal curiosity. Theodore was, on occasions, not only a fund of information and insight, on a range of scientific topics, but also a very *funny* man, whose humour belied the three-piece suit in which, we are told, he was habitually garbed.

As a poet, Stephanides was idiosyncratic to the extreme. His poetic style is highly dated, and seems to have its main affinity with the Edwardian and Georgian poets in England in the period 1900–1930. (Ian MacNiven tells us that Lawrence Durrell gave Stephanides copies of poems by Hilaire Belloc, Laurence Binyon, Walter de la Mare, John Drinkwater and Siegfried Sassoon,[15] on which Marios Byron Raizis comments that 'this is indicative of the kind of poetry that Stephanides liked to read and, of course, to try to emulate. Durrell did not attempt to make him write like Eliot, Pound, Auden, himself, nor like the current Modernists'.[16])

One might have reservations about the metre, diction and rhyming of the poems, but there are distinct characteristics which make them still rewarding. The themes which Stephanides continually revisited were: nature and natural phenomena (both in the romantic sense and with his scientist's eye); the interaction between landscape and love; and the absurdity of human behaviour. Many of his observations of London-at-night are particularly touching, but some of his most affective poems are the shortest – his 'quatrains' and 'distichs': what Lawrence Durrell would have called 'squibs', deflating pomposity and arrogance, especially in relation to politicians. And there are other humorous or mischievous pieces, such as 'Prue the Prudent Vampire', the medley of 'The Wreck of the Schooner Hesperus' and 'The Tempest'. Most moving of all, perhaps – because many of these pieces were written in old age – is the realisation and acceptance of the transience of human life, and especially of human love.

---

[15] I. MacNiven, *Lawrence Durrell: A Biography* (London: Faber and Faber, 1998), p. 129.
[16] M. B. Raizis, 'Lawrence Durrell and the Greek Poets', p. 254, n. 26.

# Select Bibliography

## Poetry

*The Golden Face* (London: Fortune Press, 1965).
*Cities of the Mind* (London: Fortune Press, 1969).
*Worlds in a Crucible* (London: Mitre Press, 1973).

## Play

*Karaghiozis and the Enchanted Tree: A Modern Greek Shadow-Play Comedy* (London: *Greek Gazette*, 1979).

## Translations (*with George Katsimbalis)

*Poems by Kostes Palamas* (London: privately printed, 1925).*
*Modern Greek Poems* (London: privately printed, 1926).*
Leandros K. Palamas, *A Study of the Palm-Tree of Kostes Palamas* [lecture, 1912] (Athens: Estia, 1931).*
C.P. Cavafy, 'Waiting for the Barbarians', with Lawrence Durrell, *New English Weekly*, 1939.
Ch. Sakellarios (ed.), *Elliniki Chori / Fifty Greek Dances* (Athens: 1940).
C. P. Cavafy, 'Thermopylae', *Symposio* 2 (Athens: 1951).*
Kostes Palamas: *Three Poems* (London: privately printed, 1969).*
Kostes Palamas, *The Twelve Words of the Gypsy* (London: Oasis Books 1974; Memphis State University Press, 1975).*
Kostes Palamas, *A Hundred Voices* (London: privately printed, 1976).
Kostes Palamas, *The King's Flute* (Athens: Kostes Palamas Institute, 1982).*
Vitzentzos Kornaros: *Erotocritos* (Athens: Papazissis Publishers, 1984).

[TRANSLATIONS, CONTINUED]

Kostes Palamas, 'Iambs and Anapaests' and 'Ascraeus' in Theofanis Stavrou and Constantine Trypanis (eds), *Kostis Palamas: A Portrait and an Appreciation* (Minneapolis: Nostos, 1985).*

HISTORY

'A Synoptic History of Corfu' in John Forte (ed.), *Corfu: Venus of the Isles* (Essex: East Essex Gazette, 1963).

SCIENTIFIC

*The Microscope and the Practical Principles of Observation* (London: Faber and Faber, 1947; revised edn 1951).

'A Survey of the Freshwater Biology of Corfu and of Certain Other Regions of Greece', *Praktika of the Hellenic Hydrobiological Institute* 2/2 (1948), pp. 11–263.

'Some Notes on the Entomostraca of Corfu, Greece, after an Interval of 23 Years', *Praktika of the Hellenic Hydrobiological Institute* 7/2 (1960), pp. 3–10.

'The Influence of the Antimosquito Fish, *Gambusia afferis*, on the Natural Fauna of a Corfu Lakelet', *Praktika of the Hellenic Hydrobiological Institute* 9 (1964), pp. 3–6.

MEMOIRS

*Climax in Crete* (London: Faber and Faber, 1946), foreword by Lawrence Durrell.

*Island Trails* (London: Macdonald, 1973), introduction by Gerald Durrell.

'In Egypt after the Fall of Crete', ed. James A. Brigham and Ian S. MacNiven, *Deus Loci* 3/3 (1980).

[MEMOIRS, CONTINUED]

'Days at Palaeocastritsa', ed. James A. Brigham, *Deus Loci* 6/6 (1983).

'First Meeting with Lawrence Durrell' and 'The House at Kalami', ed. James A. Brigham and Ian S. MacNiven, *Deus Loci* I/1 (1977); republished ed. Ian S. MacNiven and Carol Pierce, *Twentieth Century Literature* 33/3 (1987).

CORRESPONDENCE

*Lettres à Lawrence Durrell (1961–1982)*, ed. and tr. Barbara Papastavrou-Koroniatakis (Paris: Presses Universitaires de Paris 10, 2006), preface by Corinne Alexandre-Garner.

HUMOUR

'Bishop's Move', ed. James A. Brigham, *Deus Loci* 6/6 (1983).

# Corfu Memoirs

# First Meeting with Lawrence Durrell Building of the House at Kalami (Top Floor)[17]

In the late autumn of 1934 I was hunting one afternoon for mushrooms in the olive woods around Analypsis and Kanoni, a region of Corfu where *Psalliota campestris* (Field mushroom) and *Psalliota arvensis* (Horse mushroom) were very plentiful. I suddenly came upon a thin and very tall young man with a short dark-brown beard and a very pleasant face. He asked me in English what I was doing and seemed to take it just as a matter of course when I answered in the same language. We immediately struck up an acquaintance and a friendship which was to last until George Wilkinson's (for that was his name) death in the winter of 1968. On that occasion we continued the walk together and George afterwards invited me to tea at the little villa he was living in on the road from Corfu town to Kanoni. He introduced me also to his wife, Pamela, a pretty blonde whom he had just married before leaving England.[18]

It was George who first spoke to me of his friends, the Durrells, whom he hoped to persuade to come and live in Corfu. Sure enough, early in the summer of 1935, George and Pam invited me to lunch and afterwards we all three walked to the Villa Agazini, where the Durrells (who had just lately arrived in Corfu) lived, in time for tea.

The Villa Agazini (the 'Strawberry-Pink Villa' of Gerald Durrell's *My Family and Other Animals*) was situated just above the road from Perama to Benitsa [Benitses] about 4 kilometres

---

[17] In the original typescript this heading occurs before the fourth paragraph, the first three paragraphs being without a heading.

[18] Lawrence and Nancy Durrell and George and Pamela Wilkinson were close friends and shared a cottage in Sussex prior to the Wilkinsons' moving to Corfu, followed by the newly married Durrells, and subsequently the Durrell family. Characters based on George and Pamela Wilkinson appear in Durrell's first novel, *Pied Piper of Lovers* (London: Cassell, 1935; Victoria, BC: ELS Editions, 2008, ed. James Gifford).

south of Corfu town. After a very pleasant tea, I was introduced to the Durrell clan, which included old Mrs. Louisa Durrell, Leslie, Margaret and Gerald; also Roger, a large and friendly black dog of rather uncertain pedigree.

Lawrence and Nancy turned up soon after tea. I do not remember now if they were actually living in the somewhat cramped quarters of the Villa Agazini or if they still had a room for themselves at the 'Pension Suisse' in town.[19] What first struck me on meeting Lawrence was his jauntiness and self-assurance (a quality I have always lacked); also his bubbling energy. He seemed to be in every corner of the little house at once, throwing off advice and suggestions like a machine gun and arranging to undertake everything from the arrangement of the furniture to the planting of the garden.[20]

It was this abounding energy and self-assurance which always seemed to me the keynote of Lawrence's character. From the very beginning he was determined to become a great writer. He was quite certain that he would be one and, after I had known him for a short while, I was equally convinced that he would succeed in his aim.

A month or two after I knew them, the Durrell family, including Lawrence and Nancy, all transferred to the much larger Villa Anemoyanni (Gerald's 'Daffodil-Yellow Villa') situated on the coast road about 4 kilometres north of Corfu town, at a place called Sotiriotissa near Govino (Gouvia) Bay. This delightful villa was situated in extensive and almost completely wild grounds planted with cypress and olive trees

---

[19] Contrary to Gerald Durrell's *My Family and Other Animals*, Lawrence and Nancy did not live with the rest of the Durrell family and arrived on the island prior to them. Nancy does not appear in Gerald's works, nor does the Durrell family appear in Lawrence's. They did, however, visit Mrs Durrell and the rest of the family, as TS's descriptions make clear.

[20] The description of Lawrence echoes Gerald Durrell's cameo of his brother in *My Family and Other Animals*: 'designed by Providence to go through life like a small, blond firework, exploding ideas in other people's minds, and then curling up with catlike unctuousness and refusing to take any blame for the consequences' (*Corfu Trilogy*, pp. 11–12).

and thickly overgrown with clumps of arbutus and other shrubs. Larry and Nancy had a bright and airy room with two large windows partly shaded in summer by a climbing vine which covered part of one side of the house. In a very short while this room became cluttered up with typewriters (really only one), books, dictionaries, files and manuscript sheets which, as usual, soon overflowed into every nook and corner. Lawrence and his mother were always locked in a perpetual battle. She was always determined that she really must tidy up his room and Lawrence was equally determined that she should not. An example of an irresistible force encountering an immovable obstacle!

But it was not a case of all work and no play with Lawrence – not by any means. Besides boating and sea-bathing whenever the seasons permitted (or even when they didn't) Lawrence was always ready, and eager, to join in any kind of boisterous game, the rougher the better. There was a little wooded knoll at one end of the grounds which we had christened 'the fort'. We would often divide ourselves into two opposing 'armies'; one consisting (say) of Lawrence, Leslie and one of the local gardener's sons, and the other of Gerald, myself and the gardener's other son and the other side trying to storm the 'fort'. For weapons we had long feathery cypress boughs which could give a stinging but not harmful blow (sticks, of course, were not allowed) and for missiles we had cypress cones and clods of dry friable earth which burst on impact like a bomb. The cypress cones were old ones which were fairly light and we were not supposed to aim at the face, but occasionally accidents (none serious) did happen, and we all of us, including Lawrence, did turn up at tea with a bruise or two or even a black eye. But I can still remember with a thrill after all those years how we all enjoyed tearing around, shouting and yelling and throwing cypress cones and earth clods at each other – although Lawrence was twenty-four and I forty years old at the time! I wonder if Lawrence Durrell's many admirers could picture such an undignified scene *now*! And what is more, some of Lawrence's friends, who came out to Corfu from time to time, would suddenly find themselves conscripted into one of the contesting armies and plunged into a battle when they had expected a quiet cup of tea under a vine-covered trellis. I think that some of them did not show the same enthusiasm that we ourselves did.

Some time early in 1936, Lawrence and Nancy and I were invited to spend the day at the house of Mrs. Gennatas at Kouloura on the east coast some fourteen kilometres north of Corfu Town as the crow flies, but very much longer by road.

Spyros Chalikiopoulos (Spyros the Chauffeur) drove us there in his battered, but very serviceable, old American car – a Cadillac if I remember right.[21] The road was very bad and we were bumped up and down like peas in a saucepan, but the scenery was one of the most beautiful in Corfu with the blue Ionian on our right and the abrupt rocks of 900 metres high Mt. Pantokrator on our left. It was a beautiful spring day and Mrs. Gennatas' house was looking its best. It was a very old one-storied building, a Venetian look-out fortalice in the old days, with immensely thick walls which had formerly been loopholed for defence, but which were now pierced by wide French windows opening out on a wide stone terrace overlooking the sea.[22] The small, almost circular bay from which the little fishing village got its name (Kouloura = ring) lay in front of us crowded with small fishing *caïques* and rowboats. We were served a real old-fashioned tea with seed cake (but no muffins) and delicious village-made brown bread and some excellent local honey. The milk was goat's, as there was no pasture for cows in the rocky north part of the island, but that made the meal all the more interesting in spite, or rather because, of the unusual flavour. Afterwards we sat and chatted with old Mrs. Gennatas who, curious to say, spoke English with a slight Liverpool accent – I don't know if she herself had

---

[21] Spiros' car, according to Gerald Durrell, was in fact a Dodge. Spiros' nickname was 'Amerikanos', as he had lived many years in the USA.

[22] The house is described by Mildred Flamburiari, 'The Grand Old Estates' in Spiros Flamburiari (ed.), *Corfu: The Garden Isle* (London: John Murray, 1994), pp. 77–81.

ever lived in that town or if she had learnt her English from someone who had. Anyway she was able to give us many details and anecdotes of the Corfu she had known as a child. It was with regret that we left and were driven back by Spyros who was able to pick his way along the road more by the bright moonlight than by his ancient and rather dim head lights.

The upshot of this excursion was that Lawrence and Nancy were so delighted with the countryside around Kouloura that they decided that they would rent a couple of rooms in some peasant cottage there at the earliest opportunity. 'And what's more', announced Lawrence, 'it will be much easier to work there in peace and quiet than where I am now surrounded by a pack of brats who are all the time rushing about and yelling their heads off!'

Spyros the Chauffeur, ever resourceful, announced that he knew everybody around Kouloura and that he would soon find a suitable house. 'Don't you worries, Larry', he rumbled in his deep bass, 'I'll soon fixes it'. Spyros was as good as his word and some ten days later, Lawrence announced to his weeping (?) family that he and Nancy were going to live by themselves in two rooms that Spyros had found for them in a peasant house on the sea at Kalami. Kalami was a tiny fishing village of only some four or five cottages (at that time) separated from Kouloura only by a jutting headland. Lawrence and Nancy had inspected the place a few days previously and declared themselves satisfied. Kalami had all the advantages of solitude without being *too* much cut off. A rough, but passable, path connected it to the main road, and thus to Spyros and his car. Also, about one-and-a-half kilometres to the south, was a slightly larger fishing village, Agni, also connected by a path, where twice a week, weather permitting, a small diesel-engined *caïque* would arrive from Corfu Town and return the same day. This *caïque* would even sometimes call at Kalami 'on request' and transport furniture or any other bulky objects that the Durrells might have bought in town.

I stayed several times with Lawrence and Nancy at Kalami and I can even pin-point one of these visits by looking up my astronomical notebook: it was from the 2nd to the 29th August 1936. It was from their Kalami house that I made most of my observations of Peltier's Comet.[23]

The house that Spyros had found for the Durrells was the largest one in Kalami and belonged to Athenaios and his wife Eleni. Athenaios was a slight, rather pale man (from my recollection) with dark hair, a small dark moustache and a very quiet, composed and polite manner. I don't think I ever saw him excited or put out during the time that I knew him. His wife also looked rather like him both in physique and manners. She generally wore dark working peasant clothes with a white coif round her head; whilst her husband generally appeared in his shirt-sleeves with a dark grey (if I remember right) shirt and trousers. Both of them usually went about bare foot or in thick hob-nailed village-made shoes. I do not remember what Athenaios' work was. He seemed to be able to do everything from building a house to laying down night-lines and lobster pots.

The house itself was very solidly built, most of it from stone from the beach, and whitewashed a brilliant white. Athenaios claimed to have built most of it himself and I think that this was true. It was one-storied (at that period) and built on a cluster of rocks, the largest of which formed a sort of flat plateau about 10 or 15 feet above sea level (tides are negligible in the Mediterranean and Ionian Seas). The house was built on this plateau and was surrounded on nearly three sides by the sea.[24] Athenaios had also built a kind of davit from which hung the small boat he used for his fishing. The boat looked rather rough and ready and it is quite possible that he had built it also.

The house was quite roomy inside and possessed at least 3 bedrooms, a kitchen, a dining-room and a quite respectable loo

---

[23] The comet had been discovered by an American amateur astronomer, Leslie C. Peltier, earlier that year. The observation of the comet is further described below in the section 'Lawrence Durrell and Nature'.

[24] The White House has been written about several times by Lawrence Durrell and a number of other authors. It still stands in Kalami.

– something which quite surprised me for a peasant house. The Durrells had rented two of the three bedrooms (one for sleeping and the other for working) with rights to the kitchen and dining-room where we used all to meet sometimes in the evening together with any other of the villagers who cared to drop in. On these occasions Eleni would brew innumerable tiny cups of Turkish coffee and Athenaios would hand around little glasses of wine or *ouzo* (currant alcohol flavoured with aniseed). Lawrence and Nancy would generally hand around something out of a tin (biscuits, chocolate etc.) which, in those days, was a much appreciated novelty. English cigarettes were also much appreciated, though gin or whiskey did not ring the bell. Most of the guests, however, brought a bottle of wine from their own particular vineyard so that drinkables were usually more than sufficient. At first my services as interpreter were rather in demand, but it was amazing how soon Lawrence and Nancy picked up Greek. On subsequent visits I discovered that they understood the local brand of patois better than I did myself![25]

It was lucky that these 'salons' were not too frequent, as otherwise Lawrence's search for 'peace and quiet' would have been defeated. But, on the whole, except for the sound of the sea and the distant crow of a village cock, one could not have found a quieter place. Athenaios, Eleni and their daughter (about twelve years old if my memory is correct) were quietness itself. I do not know where they slept. During my visits they must have taken up their abode in one of the outhouses or sheds or gone to live with some neighbour, as they used to insist on my occupying the third room which had not been rented by the Durrells.

---

[25] Lawrence Durrell's Greek has been praised by Kimon Friar as well, and he was offered by Tambimuttu the opportunity to translate Nikos Kazantzakis' *The Odyssey: A Modern Sequel*. When he declined, it was subsequently translated by Friar. Durrell was also first in his class in Ancient Greek. His translation/adaptation of Emmanuel Royidis' *Pope Joan*, however, used a French translation as a bridge since the original text is in a complex *katharevousa* – the archaising 'purist' form that was the official language of Greek state until 1976, when it was superseded by demotic Greek.

I can still remember very vividly the lovely summer nights when a sea breeze had cooled the air and we sat on the rocks just above the sea, looking up at the bright stars and listening to the low rustle of the waves all around us. On such occasions we would talk and give our opinions on every subject under the sun. Or else we would just sit and think and soak in the feeling of the night. It was probably on one of those occasions that Lawrence thought of the idea of having an extra storey built to the house so that he could still enjoy a similar experience when the weather grew too cold to sit in the open. And also, no doubt, so as to have more room for his ever-accumulating books and manuscripts which already threatened to crowd him right out of the house and home.

With Lawrence's usual exuberance, he immediately put this proposition to Athenaios who did not seem very enthusiastic at first. But Lawrence swept him off his feet with a flood of arguments. Pointing out that *he* would make all the architectural plans, that *he* would help in the building and that *he* would pay all the expenses so that Athenaios would remain in the end with a *brand new* upper floor to his house at absolutely no cost to himself. Lawrence, of course, knew absolutely nothing about architecture or house-building and his bank balance (in those far-off days) would not have caused a tax-collector to leap with joy, but his sublime self-assurance triumphed over all obstacles. Soon he had convinced Athenaios and, on one of my subsequent visits, I found that the work of building the new upper storey had actually begun. I do not know if Lawrence had drawn up any plans, but Athenaios did not seem to need them as he could, apparently, get on all right by rule of thumb. With the aid of one of his cronies from the village and a small boy, who seemed to do nothing else but carry pails of water, Athenaios performed wonders and the floor seemed almost to grow before our eyes.

I do not know if Lawrence did much manual labour, but he certainly buzzed around with plenty of suggestions and advice. He repeatedly told Athenaios 'I want two *big* windows that will take up almost the whole of the wall facing the sea. I *insist* on two *big* windows. I *must* have two *big* windows so that I can look out on the sea and feel as if I were actually riding the waves. Two *big* windows, mind you, each one must extend from here to here. See, I'm marking it so that there should be no mistake. Two *big* wide windows. If I don't have two *big* windows, I shall just get up and leave and you'll never see me again!'

Each time Athenaios would explain, very gently and patiently, that two *big* windows would be delightful for the summer. But as soon as winter came with an icy east wind blowing over the snow-clad mainland mountains, the occupants of the upper storey would freeze. Also, during winter storms, waves were sometimes blown right against the house walls and big windows would soon be stove in. But Lawrence waved this specious excuse aside. He had to have *big* windows, or else – Athenaios ceased to argue.

At about this time, Lawrence and Nancy left Kalami for some time. I even think that they left Corfu for several months and that they went to Paris.[26] Anyway, he left strict instructions with Athenaios about the *big* windows as the extra floor was scheduled to be ready for occupation on his return. When the pair returned to Corfu, I drove out with them in Spyros' car to see them in their long expected new home. As we descended by the winding mountain path we could see in the distance that the house was ready with its extra storey all white-washed and tile roofed. I marvelled how Athenaios could have accomplished all that work in such a short time – it was clear that he did not belong to any trade-union. We finally reached the beach and could see part of the seaward side of the house. Then a roar of rage burst from Lawrence when it became evident that, although Athenaios had been worsted in *argument*, he had had the advantage of carrying out the *work* of building. The

---

[26] Lawrence and Nancy were in Paris (with short visits to London and Innsbruck) from August 1937 to April 1938: see B. Chamberlin, *A Chronology of the Life and Times of Lawrence Durrell Homme de Lettres* (Corfu: Durrell School of Corfu, 2007) pp. 19–22.

seaward aspect of the upper storey had two *small* windows!

I have rarely seen Lawrence more indignant and upset. At first he wanted to turn right around and return to the car and leave Kalami for ever. It was with great difficulty that Nancy and I persuaded him to change his mind. But for many weeks, even after the upper floor had been made into a beautiful and comfortable home, he would scarcely speak to Athenaios. But they made it up after the first few *real* autumn gales had amply proved that Athenaios' point of view had not been absolutely wrong and that it was extremely problematical if the upper floor could have been lived in if the two *big* windows had been actually installed.

Incidentally, I learnt later that Gerald's menagerie of scorpions (see *My Family and Other Animals*) and other fearsome creatures was one of the causes of Lawrence's decision to live in the far north of the island – the farther the better. It was, he said, the episode of the leeches that finally broke his nerve. I had helped Gerald one afternoon to collect some medicinal leeches (*Hirudo medicinalis*) which he took home in a wide-mouthed glass jar. These were magnificent specimens, about 75 mm (3 inches) long, with a bright longitudinal red and green stripe on each side of the body. The next day, unfortunately, this jar got knocked off the table and broken. The leeches disappeared and could not be found anywhere. Lawrence gave me a harrowing description of how he lay awake night after night feeling leeches crawling all over him and expecting to find the bedsheets drenched with crimson blood in the morning.[27] Had I known of the tragedy at the time, I could have reassured him. Out of its usual element, the medicinal leech shrivels up and dies within an hour or less. It could not have roamed about the house unless the rooms were more or less under water. A condition which most people would no doubt have noticed even if the question of leeches had never arisen.

---

[27] Leeches also appear in descriptions of Durrell's Indian childhood in *Pied Piper of Lovers*.

# The 'Ionian Banquets'

Among the many literary friends whom Lawrence Durrell made in Corfu were Zarian[28] (I can't remember his Christian name), an American–Armenian writer who had spent several years in the island with his wife and his small son, and Dr. Constantine Palatianos. The latter, who was then in his late sixties or early seventies, was a man of great erudition, belonging to a very old Corfiot family. He had a very deep knowledge of English and Greek literature. He was, at that time, engaged in writing a history of Corfu with special reference to the Venetian occupation. This work was unfortunately interrupted by World War II and his death in 1944 and, as far as I know, has remained in manuscript only.

Mr. Zarian and Dr. Palatianos, together with Lawrence Durrell and a few other lovers of literature, whose names I do not now remember, organised towards the end of 1936 (or early in 1937) the 'Ionian Banquets'. In spite of their great age difference Lawrence Durrell and Dr. Palatianos got on very well together, and, in my opinion, the composite figure of Count D. in *Prospero's Cell* owes more to Dr. Palatianos than to any other person. I have often wondered if this was deliberate or sub-conscious on Lawrence's part. In any case the portrait is an excellent one. They formed a small literary club with a very modest entrance fee and once a fortnight all the members (about thirty) met at the Perdika Restaurant in the centre of town. The intention was to found a small locally printed literary journal to which all the members would contribute; but, for various reasons, including the departure from Corfu of some of the members and the increasingly unsettled world

---

[28] Gostan Zarian (1885–1969) was an Armenian novelist and autobiographer who lived in Corfu 1935–38. Durrell wrote an essay, 'Constant Zarian: Triple Exile' and a lengthy portion of their correspondence has been published in an edited version by Vartan Matiossian as 'Kostan Zarian and Lawrence Durrell: A Correspondence', *Journal of the Society for Armenian Studies* 8 (1995), pp. 75–101.

situation, no number of this journal was ever printed. The 'banquets', however, took place and continued for over a year with great success. Then they also were gradually abandoned; I do not now recall why, but the world situation probably had much to do with this.

When at their height, the 'Ionian Banquets' went with a swing, and were greatly enjoyed by all present. The 'Perdika' (Partridge) Restaurant was a low old building dating probably from Venetian times or, at latest, from the beginning of the nineteenth century.[29] It had a low vaulted basement, very cool in summer, which had perhaps been a wine-cellar in its time, but which was now used for special occasions. This basement was reserved on the nights of the 'Ionian Banquets' and, on those occasions, its only furniture was a long plank table on trestles and the requisite number of picturesque, though rather hard, rush-bottomed chairs of exactly the same pattern as the celebrated picture of Van Gogh.

At these banquets, after an opening speech by Mr. Zarian, who had constituted himself master-of-the-ceremonies, various toasts were drunk and the dinner eaten amid much animated noise and clamour all the guests apparently speaking at once. Afterwards came the after-dinner speeches at which Lawrence Durrell was often called upon to oblige. His little impromptu answers were short and usually very much to the point. He spoke in English (which was understood by practically all those present) and he had a way of unexpectedly interjecting remarks in colloquial Greek which he had picked up with amazing rapidity. These little speeches – including the remarks – always had great success, especially if the latter were of a ribald flavour.

The proprietor of 'The Perdika' was an excellent cook and always took pride in surpassing himself at these banquets. The

---

[29] The taverna was located on a *parodos* (cross-street) of N. Theotoki Street, leading from the Esplanade to the Spilia or old city gate by the (Old) Port; it was destroyed during bombardments in the Second World War and has been replaced by modern buildings.

wine also was good – at least so I have been told by the others as I have absolutely no palate for wine. To me all wines taste the same, except that some are sweet and some are sour.

After the after-dinner speeches, members would sometimes give a little talk on some literary subject or read out a short poem or essay. Then came the election of any new member who might wish to be elected. For this Mr. Zarian had composed a very special ceremony. I am able to give it in full as, by some miracle, a copy of it has remained in my possession.

*Banquets Ioniens*
*Cérémonie – Questionnaire*

Alors que les membres fondateurs entourés des membres permanents se rangent à la tête de la table les attitudes solennels, le nouveau désirant s'approche lentement, les mains croiseés sur la poitrine et la tête baisée en signe d'humiliation, s'incline trois fois, prend un verre de la table et frappe doucement deux fois sur la table et une fois contre la bouteille et dit d'une voix suppliante:

'Oh sérénissime, faites que j'y sois de la compagnie!'

'Et pourquoi, homme, voulez vous y être parmi cet haut Aréopage? Est-ce par un interêt bas ou êtes vous poussé par une idealité suprême?'

'C'est par cette dernière, car là je vois la sagesse extrême de la vie.'

'Vous bouvez le rouge ou le blanc?'

'Ni rouge, ni blanc, mais ce nectar dont la couleur appartient plus au soleil qu'à la terre, dont l'esprit l'émane des forêts et dont le goût rapelle celui de ce fin nectar dont les dieux s'abreuvaient sur l'Olympe!'

(Les membres fondateurs repètent en coeur le mot '*rétsina*' tandis que quelqu'un vers le premier verre et l'un des membres fondateurs dit 'Vos voeux exaucés, et, par le pouvoir de Bacchus et des dieux des '*mézes*' nous vous nommons membre permanent.' Alors tout le monde crie '*Zito!*')

Le premier jour le nouveau membre doit faire l'éloge en paroles poétiques et en un style allégorique du 'chant solaire' et PAYER TROIS BOUTEILLES.

*Ionian Banquets*
*Ceremony and Questionnaire*

While the founding members, surrounded by the permanent members, seat themselves at the head of the table in solemn attitudes, the new candidate for election advances slowly, with hands crossed on his breast and eyes downcast in sign of humility. He bows three times, takes a tumbler from the table and, tapping it softly twice on the table and once against the bottle, repeats in a voice of supplication:

'Deign, Oh High-born, to accept me as one of the company.'

'And why, O man, do you wish to join this Areopagus? Is it from base motives or are you fired by a supreme Idealism?'

'It is because of the latter. For there do I see the highest wisdom of Life'.

'Do you drink white wine or red?'

'Neither the one nor the other, but that nectar whose colour belongs more to the sun than to the earth, whose soul emanates from the forests and whose taste recalls the delicate nectar that refreshed the gods on Olympus.'

(The founding members intone in chorus the word '*rétsina*', whilst someone pours out the first glass and one of the founding members recites 'Your wish is fulfilled and, by the power conferred on us by Bacchus and by the gods of the '*mézes*', we name you permanent member.' Then all present cry '*Zito!*')

The first day the new member must toast the 'Solar Hymn' in a poetical and allegorical speech and PAY FOR THREE BOTTLES.

The enthusiastic references to '*rétsina*' (resinated wine), one of Lawrence Durrell's favourite beverages, makes me think that he played his part in composing the above 'Ceremony and Questionnaire'.

'*Mézes*' – small hors-d'oeuvres which are usually served with '*rétsina*' and other drinks.

'Zito' – the Greek equivalent of 'long *live*' or 'hurrah'. The best translation of 'Zito' *is* 'long live' as it is usually (but not always) followed by… the King,… the Republic, or whatever.

# Lawrence Durrell and Nature

Lawrence Durrell was always greatly interested in anything to do with Nature; not so much, I think, from the strictly scientific view as he was from his love of beauty. His artist's eye was always noticing the way that Nature always managed to harmonise with itself. He would often gather big bunches of the wild flowers which were so abundant in Spring and Autumn around Kalami and point out to me that their bright colours never seemed to clash as would be the case with artificial dyes in a tapestry or a carpet. The wild flowers were always a great delight to him and to his wife, Nancy.

Lawrence had noticed early in his stay in Corfu that there were two kinds of local cypress trees. Some stood up straight with short branches closely pressed to the trunk like 'tapering black flames' as he put it; whilst others had longer branches spread out at angles rather like ordinary fir trees. He asked me early on if the peasants were right in saying that the straight cypresses were male trees and the spread ones female. I explained that this was not the case. The cypress is monoecious, but occurs in two varieties, *Cupressus sempervirens* var. *stricta* (the upright kind) and *Cupressus sempervirens* var. *horizontalis*. Lawrence Durrell much preferred the former variety as, owing to their slim shape and very dark – sometimes almost black – colour, 'they made such a perfect foil to the tortuous grey-green olives', those other characteristic trees of the Corfu landscape. Even in those early days he would make innumerable rough scribbles and sketches of what he saw around him, always trying to catch a new facet of the ever-changing scene. But he was never satisfied with these sketches which he tore up almost as soon as he completed them.

One morning in October 1936, Lawrence showed me, in great excitement, a huge beetle that he had found on the sea shore at Kalami a few days before. It was still living when he picked it up, but it died very shortly afterwards. It certainly was an extraordinary looking insect, rather scorpion-like in shape and somewhat resembling the common European water scorpion or *Nepa*. It was the largest insect I had ever seen, as it measured 81 mm (nearly 3¼ inches) in length. I was quite as excited about it as Durrell was, as I thought it might be a new species — nothing like it was depicted in any of the books I had read on European insects. With Lawrence's permission, I sent the specimen to the Vienna Natural History Museum and soon got back the answer that the creature was a *Belostoma niloticum* Stål (*Lethocerus cordofanus* Mayr) from N.E. Africa and had never before been recorded in Europe. Since that date, this insect has been recorded in several other parts of S.E. Europe, though still very rare. Lawrence's younger brother, Gerald, found two more specimens, both dead, in the sea near the Corfu village of Kondokali in December 1937; and two more specimens, dead, were again found in the summer of 1967.[30] But, if the Vienna Museum is right, Lawrence Durrell can claim to be the first to have observed *Belostoma niloticum* in Europe.

Lawrence's interest in Nature extends also to astronomy, and the stars often enter into his writings and especially his poetry. I stayed with Lawrence and Nancy in their Kalami house from the 2nd to the 29th August 1936. I was able during that period to show them both the first comet they had ever seen. For a few days following the 7th August (before that date the moon, near its full, had been too bright) the comet was well visible to the eye as a tiny oval blur with a short straight tail about four degrees long. With my Zeiss prism binoculars X5 it was quite striking for someone who had never seen a comet before. Seated on the warm sun-baked rocks near the house, we observed it with great interest in the clear Corfu sky far from any interfering town lights. Lawrence made the comet the subject of a poem which he promised to show me when

---

[30] In 1967, Stephanides revisited Corfu for the first time since World War II in order to assist Gerald Durrell in making the documentary film *Corfu, Garden of the Gods*. He had corresponded with Lawrence Durrell during his returns to Corfu only a few years earlier. While staying in Corfu, Gerald stayed in an apartment on the top floor of an imposing mansion on the city walls, on Arseniou St, owned by Theodore's younger sister.

completed to his satisfaction. But he was never quite satisfied – so I never saw it. I have not seen it either in any of his published poems, so I am afraid that it must have been destroyed with other *juvenilia*. A pity!

Lawrence was particularly fascinated with all kinds of sea life, both plant and animal. He and Nancy (and I when I happened to be visiting them) would spend hours exploring the rocks and shallow waters all round Kalami. Sometimes we would take a boat, either on our own or as the guest of some fisherman in our neighourhood, and explore further afield. There was a group of flat rocks at the foot of a low limestone cliff a little to the north of Kouloura which was a great favourite of ours, and which Lawrence had christened 'Fig Tree Point'. A thick and evidently very old fig tree grew out of the base of this cliff and its wide leaves covered the landward end of the rocks like a tent. It was cool and dark in this 'tent' and we used to take some provisions with us and have our midday meal there after a long sea bathe. There were some shallower areas there where the sun could warm the sea until it was almost like a hot bath whilst, nearby, a current would keep the sea almost icy cold. Lawrence particularly enjoyed the contrast of these different temperatures which, he claimed, 'stimulated his brain'. I, myself, preferred the warmer water. Incidentally, many of the white stones near the fig tree rocks produced a kind of white lather when vigorously rubbed with sea water. Lawrence and Nancy enjoyed rubbing their skins with one of these stones and then plunging into the sea. I was never able to discover why the stones at just this spot produced this effect. This did not happen elsewhere along the coast.

Sometimes Lawrence would take a very battered old typewriter, swathed in an old mackintosh to protect it (more or less) from rust and do a bit of typing under the fig tree. He said that this also stimulated him and that he had typed quite a lot of *The Black Book* in this manner. But I noticed that the typewriter usually fought a losing battle against the lure of the sea. Lawrence was soon back again in the water.

In fact I often wondered if Lawrence Durrell had invented some kind of time-machine which enabled him to squeeze more hours into the day than the usual twenty-four. His energy seemed prodigious, he was always on the go (except for a post-prandial siesta which could be long or short as he chose – though, usually, he chose it long), and it seemed to me that he never left himself time to touch his typewriter. Yet touch it he most certainly did, as was evidenced by the pages and pages of typescript piled up on his writing table and spilling over onto the floor and over everything else in his room – and in fact the whole house. Nancy, who acted as his secretary (besides being an excellent cook and also finding time for some lovely water colour paintings of her own) must have found it a hard job to keep track of the pages as Lawrence just seemed to shoot them out of his typewriter anywhere – often enough on the floor.

Lawrence had the happy knack of being able to compose his works straight onto the typewriter and at tremendous speed. He only used two fingers, but they seemed able to keep up with the gush of his ideas and would have to fill in such finicky things as articles and punctuation marks by hand afterwards. But his final drafts were always very neat – whether it was he or Nancy who typed out these final drafts I do not know. Lawrence also had the equally useful knack of being able to pick up or set down a piece of work at will. From what I remember, he could suddenly dash off in the middle of a conversation, work hard at his typewriter for ten minutes or more, and then return and continue the conversation as if he had never broken it off. In those days at least (I don't know afterwards) he seemed to be able to turn a tap in his brain on and off at will. In this way he was able to combine great zest and enjoyment of life with great industry – and that without seeming to appear industrious. Sometimes I would wake up at two or three in the morning and hear the faint, distant click of his typewriter in his room. Was he an early riser? Yes, when he felt like it. But not if he didn't. It was at this time that a great part of *The Black Book* was written. Lawrence read me a lot of it and I remember how I enjoyed the ghost story of the sarcophagus which he reserved for a moonlit night.[31]

Lawrence Durrell always enjoyed good food, and here he was lucky in having Nancy who was a real *cordon-bleu* and who could turn out any kind of dish, whether English or Greek, with the most rudimentary materials and utensils. He was not a 'finicky' eater, but the food had to be *good*; and he could content himself with a local peasant wine, but that, too, had to be of good quality. He soon established himself as the possessor of a discriminating palate among the local peasantry, with the result that their best wine was always reserved for him. Wine tasting in Greece in general and in Corfu in particular is very much a lottery. The art of wine-making is still very little known and the same vineyard can produce a good wine one season and an undrinkable one the next. Lawrence discovered this early on in his stay and always insisted on sampling every bottle before buying it. This had certain inconveniences if he wanted to buy more than two or three bottles at a time. Fortunately the Corfu wines are, as a rule, not heady.

Lawrence Durrell was an excellent swimmer and diver and, whenever it was warm enough, he and Nancy would spend a good deal of their time in the sea around Kalami, Mankephali and 'Fig Tree Point'. Lawrence's delight was to bring up all sorts of curiosities from the sea bottom; shells, coloured seaweeds, curiously shaped stones which were used to decorate their Kalami home. Two things particularly delighted him and Nancy; one was the pieces of drift-wood which they picked up on the beach or found floating on the sea. These pieces of wood were often highly polished by wave action and often they presented contorted and weird shapes. Lawrence would accen-

---

[31] As Stephanides notes in his letter to Brigham, which lists corrections to the typescript for this memoir, 'I am afraid that my memory has betrayed me here & that Larry read us the Sarcophagus Ghost Story from *Panic Spring*. Please verify this as I have mislaid my own copy.' This is in fact the case. See the chapter 'The Mummy' in *Panic Spring* (London: Faber and Faber, 1937, under the pseudonym Charles Norden; Victoria, BC: ELS Editions, 2008, ed. James Gifford). Both this and *The Black Book* (Paris: Obelisk Press, 1938; London: Faber and Faber, 1973) were written and set on Corfu.

tuate their weirdness by a little pen knife work and some deft touches with his coloured inks. In this way a good many extraordinary creatures: dragons, gorgons, sea monsters, would be staring at the visitor from almost every table, mantle-piece or window sill.

The other object of delight was a curious little sea weed, *Acetabularia mediterranea*, which Lawrence called 'Japanese parasols'. And in fact they *did* look like miniature parasols, two to three centimetres in diameter, pearly white underneath and pale green on top. These grew on rocks and stones, singly or in small groups, and were stiff enough to retain their shape when dry. Pebbles bearing clusters of these 'Japanese parasols' on their slender white stalks were nearly always scattered about the room.

Squids and octopuses always exercised a great repulsion–fascination for Lawrence, and he rarely refused the opportunity of going on an octopus hunt, whether by day or by night with a carbide lamp, with any of the local fishermen. He describes one of these night octopus hunts on pages 39–40 of *Prospero's Cell* (1945 edition).

Sea phosphorescence was another subject that fascinated Lawrence. This phenomenon is particularly vivid in Corfu in late August and September. He would delight then to go out by boat on a dark moonless night and watch the swirls of silver light which would stream past the prow or drip in big splashes from the oars. He would dive time after time into the dark water so as to watch the sparks of greenish white illumination that surrounded him like a nimbus.

On one of these night excursions we got, however, a little more than we bargained for. While in the water, we suddenly heard a loud hissing or snorting sound, at regular intervals of about five or six seconds, approaching us from seaward. We all scrambled hurriedly back into the boat and started in the direction of the sound, but all that we could see was a faint phosphorescent ripple in the water. The snorting approached us until it became quite weirdly loud in the darkness and then slowly receded again and faded away. It was probably a harmless grampus[32] (the expression 'snorting like a grampus' is well known), but we decided to be on the safe side and we did no more swimming that night.

On another occasion, Lawrence, Nancy and I had just finished our midday picnic meal and were lounging on the rocks near Mankephali. Suddenly we heard loud feminine shrieks from just around a rocky promontory. We all three rushed there and saw a group of five or six village girls who had been having a sea bathe – more or less fully clothed as was their modest habit. One of these girls, who apparently could not swim, had got out of her depth and was in difficulties. Her companions, whether they could swim or not, had promptly panicked and were just running up and down the beach screaming. Lawrence promptly dived in and dragged the victim to shore. She had lost consciousness – but more from fright than drowning, as she recovered her senses after a few minutes after we had given her a little artificial respiration.

Lawrence was, naturally, the hero of the hour and his reputation and prestige among the local inhabitants rose very considerably (Summer 1937).

---

[32] A large species of dolphin typically weighing 300 kg, not to be confused with the orca.

# Days at Palaeocastritsa

In late April of 1937 I rented three rooms in a small one-storied cottage belonging to a peasant who owned a small plot of land planted with olive trees on the shore of the southmost of the three bays of Palaeocastritsa.[33] Lawrence and Nancy rented the remaining three rooms. The peasant and his family lived in a small farm house nearby and supplied us daily with goat's milk, eggs, chickens and vegetables. Not far from us was another small cottage belonging, I believe, to the same peasant family which had been let to a young American painter named Koster – I forget his Christian name.[34] My wife, Mary, and my daughter, Alexia, then aged six, lived in this peasant cottage together with Alexia's nurse. I was not able to stay with them all the time as I worked, with my partner Dr. Philoctimon Paramythiotis, in our X-ray clinic in town, but I used to come up to Palaeocastritsa on Friday afternoons and leave early on Monday morning by the local hotel car. This latter was a large German Mercedes, almost like a small bus, which could seat about ten persons besides the driver.

In those days Palaeocastritsa was almost deserted compared to today. There were only two small hotels, one run by the government-sponsored Tourist Commission, the other a private hotel. I do not think that any villas had been built as yet.

The Spring was beautiful but rather cold that year so that, in early May, one could not remain in the sea very long, but the sun-bathing was delightful in the middle of the day. The nights and evenings were sometimes quite chilly. There was a small iron wood-stove in one of the rooms of our cottage and the Durrells, Mary and I and Koster would often sit round this chatting. Sometimes we were joined by a Mr. Lockheart,

---

[33] On the west coast of Corfu.
[34] Maurice Koster was an American painter (see I. MacNiven, *Lawrence Durrell: A Biography*, pp. 138–59).

another painter (or writer?) who lived in one of the hotels. These chats were usually combined with a kind of picnic supper cooked by Mary and Nancy and followed by hot cocoa (for Mary and I and the others, if they felt like it), or by some retsina or gin for those who liked something stronger. These conversations included every topic under the sun, but literature and art naturally came first. Lawrence supplied the literature and Koster the art. Sometimes specimens of both were read or exhibited.

It was some time in early May that Koster acquired a small motor-boat. I don't know if he had bought it or rented it, nor where it came from. But one Friday afternoon when I arrived at Palaeocastritsa I saw it floating in our bay with Koster proudly tuning up the engine (not an outboard motor) or doing something equally messy and mysterious.

She looked quite a big boat of her kind, not very fast but roomy and broad and stable. She could seat about six or possibly eight people and she was painted white, green below the water line. Koster suggested that Lawrence and I should go with him for a spin right away to try her out. It was a fine calm afternoon, with several hours before sunset, so Lawrence and I gladly accepted.

The boat was a great success, we seemed to glide over the water with her tut-tutting away without a hitch. We sped southwards parallel to Corfu's west coast. Suddenly we seemed to lose speed for no obvious reason, and, at the same time, the engine changed its steady tune to an irregular kind of coughing. Koster stopped the engine but, after a careful examination, he announced in a puzzled way that he could not find anything wrong. The only defect was that the propeller would not turn. We soon found out why. We had, all three, been so engrossed with the lovely scenery that we had failed to notice a long line of cork floating right across our bows and we had run slap into some fishing nets. These had been laid down by some of the local fishermen who evidently intended to leave them in position all night, as not a single fishing vessel was in sight anywhere.

What is more, we were just out of hailing distance of the shore and, anyway, we were opposite an uninhabited stretch with no houses visible. It was, consequently, up to us to free our boat before night-fall.

A quick search disclosed that we had only a small penknife (mine) and an ordinary dinner-knife (whose?) on board. Armed with these, Lawrence and Koster (much better swimmers than myself) went overboard and, with great difficulty, managed to hack through the stiff strands of the net and free the motor-boat. But other parts of the net had rolled themselves so tightly around the axle of the screw that, in spite of all their diving, neither Koster nor Lawrence could free it. Meanwhile night was falling, the sea was getting rougher, and a breeze from the east started to blow us away from the shore. There were no oars on board, so that the situation was beginning to get somewhat disconcerting. Fortunately, at this point we drifted past a small bay and saw two small fishing boats drawn up on the sand. No human beings were in sight, however, so now it was my turn to do something, as the two others were quite exhausted from their efforts to free the propeller. The distance was within my swimming range, luckily, so I was able to make it. But then I found that both boats were secured by short iron chains to iron staples rammed deep into the hard pebbly beach. Fortunately, although the chains were strong, the padlocks (as often happens) were old and rusty and I managed to break one with a heavy stone. I managed, too, to row back to the motor-boat in spite of the fact that the sea had become quite choppy and I am a very bad sailor. I did not feel at all sea-sick whilst rowing, but the moment I stepped into the motor-boat I was practically doubled up with sea-sickness. Fortunately both Koster and Lawrence were good sailors and they were able to tow the disabled motor-boat back to Palaeocastritsa by taking turns at the single pair of oars that our pirated row-boat contained.

We reached Palaeocastritsa a couple of hours after sunset and Lawrence and I found our respective wives practically weeping on the beach in the true tradition of the sea. We were all three rather fagged out and chilled, but a good supper by a warm stove soon put us to rights again, except for head colds which lasted us for the rest of the weekend. The fishermen whose nets we had damaged and whose row-boat we had pirated were very nice about it. The latter told us to forget it since no damage had been done except to a very old padlock and the former said that a few yards of netting would repair everything. So after a very few drachmae had changed hands and a certain number of glasses of ouzo had been downed, everything was arranged to everybody's satisfaction.

Except, perhaps, to Koster's motor boat. Her engine had been strained or her propeller shaft put out of true, anyway she was never quite the same afterwards and we never went for very long excursions in her. The engine's performance was rather erratic at times. And, anyway, the motor-boat's nose was soon put out of joint by the arrival of the magnificent *Van Norden*.

As with with the motor-boat, I don't know how or when the *Van Norden* was built or acquired. I believe that Lawrence and Nancy had her first at Kalami (they were often moving from Kalami to Palaeocastritsa and back), but I first saw her in the south Palaeocastritsa Bay one Friday afternoon when I arrived – I think it was the middle or end of July 1937. She certainly looked magnificent though, in my opinion, just a little sombre as she was a deep black all over except for a white bowsprit and a white mast. And, of course, her sails when they were unfurled, but I never saw this very often. I once suggested to Lawrence that I thought her appearance would be still more improved if she had a broad white line painted right round her just below the gunwale. Lawrence grew quite enthusiastic with the idea. He even said that he would have the line broken by six black gaps at regular intervals to look like miniature gun-ports. With a slight sea mist to confuse the eye, it would then look as if the *Van Norden* was bigger and further away than she actually was and she would consequently look like a twelve-gun sloop-of-war. Lawrence was, of course, just pulling my leg. But sometimes he would get so carried away by pulling other peoples' legs that he would end up by tweaking his own also. But this was not one of those occasions, and the *Van Norden* remained black all over.

Being one of the world's worst sailors (I can even *begin* to feel sea-sick at the cinema if a *too* rough sea is shown), I can't describe the *Van Norden* any further except to say that she had only one mast. From memory, I would say that she must have been about 20 ft. long – but I may be completely mistaken. I cannot say anything about her sailing qualities as I never myself saw her sailed anywhere. I think we were all too lazy at that time, it being the middle of summer, to screw up the necessary energy for the manual labour needed. But the anchored *Van Norden* made an excellent plaything and we would chase each other round her, or scramble aboard her and dive off again into the nice cool (but not *too* cool) waters of the bay. All of us as happy as sand-boys. (Why *are* sand-boys particularly happy?) I can't understand how Lawrence managed to get any work done. And yet he *did* manage to get through a lot, as it was during this period that he wrote *Panic Spring* and put the finishing touches to *The Black Book*.[35] But every now and then Lawrence would retire with Nancy to their more secluded and inaccessible Kalami house and I think that he did most of his work there, with Palaeocastritsa more as a rest and playground.

Incidentally, the sea in the south Palaeocastritsa Bay was very much cooler than the sea around Kalami. It was cooler, too, than the sea in the other two Palaeocastritsa bays. The local fishermen affirmed that deep freshwater springs welled up under the sea in this bay and we often wondered if they were right.

Another thing that interested Lawrence very much was that the fishermen (mainly the older ones) around Palaeocastritsa still built light coracles according to a pattern that must have remained unchanged for many thousand years – in fact probably harking back to palaeolithic times. These coracles, or 'papyrellas' as they were locally called, were about

---

[35] Durrell wrote *Panic Spring* between March and December 1935 and *The Black Book* between January 1936 and February 1937.

six or seven feet long with a pointed upturned prow and a rounded stern. The fisherman would sit on it as a horse with his legs in the water and row it with a rough wooden paddle. They were used mostly for putting down night-lines or lobster-pots and their owners claimed that they were absolutely unsinkable. They were built almost entirely of the local reed, *Arundo donax*, and another plant with a light firm pith which I was not able to recognise at the time (many years later, in 1964, Lawrence learnt from Captain Antoniou, a mutual friend, that this was *Ferula communis*); the whole seemed to be merely lashed together with strong tarred twine.

Lawrence soon picked up the knack of paddling one of these coracles and vowed that some day he would have a *de luxe* model specially built for him. Alas! When the opportunity occurred in 1964, the making of these coracles was already a dying art known only to one or two very old men, and the *de luxe* coracle was never built. Lawrence writes a graphic description of these coracles in his letter to me of June 1964 and in two post-cards, of June and July 1964.[36]

Another friend who used occasionally to drop in on us at Palaeocastritsa and who seemed much struck by Larry and Nancy (especially Nancy's water colours; he very highly praised a picture of a large white Persian cat that used to lounge about the Margaritis Milk Shop) was Réné Berlincourt, a Swiss painter who lived for several years in Corfu and only left it after World War II had broken out.

Réné Berlincourt, together with five or six other friends of his — mostly artists or writers (Swiss and Austrian, if I remember right) had pooled their not very copious funds together and had had a small *caïque* built specially for them in the small shipping yard of Mandouki, a suburb of Corfu. For

---

[36] Stephanides' portion of this correspondence and his responses to Durrell's queries on the coracles are held in the Bibliothèque Lawrence Durrell at l'Université Paris-X, Nanterre. Stephanides' sketch of the 'papyrella' coracle appears in *Lettres à Lawrence Durrell*, p. 96, with photograph on p. 103.

months Berlincourt had superintended the building with an eagle eye to make sure that copper (or was it brass?) nails were used and not iron ones that would rust, and a thousand and one other details. Finally the *caïque* was ready. 'A real beauty', said Berlincourt, 'with two small cabins and four bunks for eight people. I designed all the furnishings myself. You must all come and see them!'

For some reason or other, neither Lawrence, I, nor any of the Palaeocastritsa set were able to accept Berlincourt's invitation for the maiden voyage and the little celebration that was planned. But Berlincourt turned up again at Palaeocastritsa looking a bit crestfallen and told Lawrence and me that it was very lucky for us that we had not been able to accept his invitation. It seems, according to his account, that they had left Mandouki late in the afternoon and, as the weather was at its finest and the sea calm, they had sailed over to Paganià, a little bay on the Epirote coast just opposite Corfu.[37] This bay is completely landlocked and, accordingly, safe even in the roughest weather, so that it is a great favourite with yachtsmen. The names of yachts and other boats with dates as far back as the 1800s could still be seen (in 1937) painted on the surrounding cliffs.

A very pleasant little dinner party was enjoyed by crew and guests, some ten people in all, and the health of the *caïque* was liberally drunk. After which Berlincourt crept into his bunk – rather groggily, as he himself admitted. He was awakened in the small hours by loud shouts of 'fire!' and had only time to dash up on deck and dive overboard in his shirt as he had not bothered to put on pyjamas (did he have any?). The *caïque* was a mass of roaring flame, but fortunately nobody had been lost although several had been slightly singed. 'And thus', concluded Berlincourt, 'perished our poor *Julia*. On her maiden journey. Just like the *Titanic*!' The cause of the conflagration, incidentally, was never discovered. 'We were all a little bit elevated

---

[37] This is only slightly south of the border with Albania, directly north-east of Corfu Town.

when we retired to bed', admitted Berlincourt, 'and somebody probably dropped a lighted cigarette behind some of my beautiful hangings which I had spent weeks to design and paint'. The *caïque* was not insured and that was the end of Berlincourt and his friends' ship-building venture. They had been cleaned out financially and, anyway, World War II soon intervened.

Poor Berlincourt was not lucky, but he was a good artist. He helped Lawrence and Nancy with some of the interior decorations of the *Van Norden*. And without the latter bursting into flames as Lawrence said he half feared she might.

# At the Villa Anemoyanni

One evening in the autumn of 1936 (October I think it was) Lawrence Durrell and Nancy had left Kalami to stay for a short while with the rest of the Durrell family in the Anemoyanni Villa at Sotiriotissa. This house boasted a very large room on the ground floor which was used as a sitting-room and dining-room combined. This room was the only one in the place that contained a real fireplace and, as the night was cool, a pleasant aromatic fire of cypress and olive wood was burning in it. Lawrence was striding like a restless panther round and round the room as was his habit when thinking up plots and dialogue for his books. Suddenly his eyes fixed themselves just above the mantelpiece and he called out in a rather strained voice: 'Come here, Theodore, and tell me if I'm seeing things! What are those two objects on the wall just over there?' I came and looked. The two objects were a couple of Death's Head Hawk Moths (*Acherontia atropos*) sitting on the wall with their wings spread out flat and the gruesome white skull on their back well in evidence. I explained that these moths were fairly common in Corfu and that they often entered houses in autumn when the weather outside began to grow colder. Lawrence picked one of the moths up, but dropped it again like a hot coal when it emitted a shrill squeak like a pigmy mouse. I hastened to explain that *Acherontia* was the only European moth that could perform that little trick. 'Why didn't you tell me that before I picked the damn thing up and had it scare the life out of me!' But he rallied round after drinking a couple of ouzos, although he insisted that his heart would never beat in quite the same place again.

Another thing that I noticed about Lawrence Durrell was his extraordinary knack of being able to pick up any musical instrument and, after just a few minutes' practice, get some sort of tune out of it. I have seen him master in this way a Greek shepherd's flute and a piano-accordion belonging to the propietor of a village café.

Lawrence was equally quick in getting into the rhythm and picking up dance steps, including Greek folk dances. In this the other members of the family were also very gifted. One afternoon I brought a gramophone record of a Cretan folk dance, the *Pendozali*, which has a fast and lively step. The dancers form a circle and dance with their hands on each others' shoulders. I showed Lawrence and the others the steps and, in next to no time, we were all dancing round and round the sitting room. It happened to be a cold grey rainy day outside so we kept this up for most of the afternoon, dancing the *Pendozali* and several other Greek folk dances, the *Kalamatiano*, the *Syrtos* and the *Trata* which the whole Durrell family learnt with equal facility. We thus spent a very gay afternoon, in spite of the dismal weather and worked up a wonderful appetite for supper. The latter meal almost always included a curry, as old Mrs. Durrell had lived many years in India and was an excellent cook.[38]

---

[38] For a fictional account of the Durrells' early life in India, see Lawrence Durrell's semi-autobiographical first novel, *Pied Piper of Lovers*.

## Kalami Again

The house at Kalami was certainly in an ideal situation as it was built on a kind of plateau of flat rocks jutting into the sea in a fairly deep bay. To the south was a kind of rocky cape (Mankephali) surmounted with cypress and olive trees. Sometimes, of an evening, Lawrence, Nancy and I would sit on the still warm rocks chatting. It was on one of these occasions that Lawrence, by the light of a guttering candle, read me the Sarcophagus and footsteps episode of *The Black Book*.[39] Under these circumstances the tale was doubly gruesome, and I think that Nancy and I cast a good many shuddering glances over our shoulders into the surrounding shadows. Or simply keeping silent and, as it were, soaking in the beauty around us. We would hear the piping of a shepherd's flute from this cape. The effect in the dark or in the moonlight (the shepherd never seemed to play in the daytime) was both beautiful and eerie. Lawrence used to affirm that it was Pan himself playing as he had gone out several times and tried to stalk the player. But the piping always stopped before he could get close enough to see the player. Once or twice we did catch sight in the daytime of an oldish man leading about five or six goats and two or three sheep, but I never learnt if it was he who did the playing. I asked some of the villagers, but they said he was from the village of Agni and that they did not know his name. I can't remember now if Lawrence ever managed to speak to him.[40] One summer (in 1936, I think) we used often to be joined on our rock by a very nice American couple, Barclay and Jane Hudson, who had rented the little house on the Mankephali peninsula for the summer.[41]

---

[39] As previously noted, this is from the chapter 'The Mummy' in Lawrence Durrell's *Panic Spring*, originally published under the pseudonym Charles Norden.
[40] Compare Lawrence Durrell, *Prospero's Cell*, pp. 17–18.
[41] Barclay Hudson was responsible for introducing Lawrence Durrell to Henry Miller's *Tropic of Cancer*.

Sometimes we would all go over to the Hudsons, especially during the day, as Mankephali possessed a delightful little cove in which the water ran to a deep rich blue right up to the cliffs that surrounded it. At one spot the rocks projected in an ideal diving board over a very deep bit of water and we used to dive here to our hearts' content. There were also several other rocky 'diving boards' at various heights. I (being a bad diver) always chose the one that was only a foot or two above the sea, but Lawrence and Barclay (and Nancy and Jane also) used to jump from what were, to me, horrifying heights. After which we would lie about on the rocks to dry and to sun bathe and then either Nancy or Jane would produce a lunch basket which we soon emptied.

Those, indeed, were ideal days. The everyday world seemed very far away and I don't think that it occurred to any of us that a second World War was looming only three years ahead.

Sometimes, especially when a few friends came up from town, we would play makeshift cricket with an old tennis patch of ground among the olive trees behind the Kalami house. But there was so much broom and other bushes around the place that I think that we spent as much time (or perhaps more) hunting for the ball as hitting it. Lawrence always maintained that 'somebody' ought to go round and clear away some of those bushes. The rest of us agreed that 'somebody' ought to do it, but, when it came to the point, that 'somebody' never materialised. The work appeared too uninteresting – too much like *work* in fact.

In 1937 (either in late August or early September) Lawrence and Nancy left the house at Kalami to spend some weeks in Paris. They stayed, if I remember right, at a place called *Villa Seurat*, and it was there that they met the American writer, Henry Miller who, at that time, was still very little known.[42] Lawrence and Henry got on very well together and

---

[42] For an account of the Durrells' visit to Villa Seurat, see I. MacNiven, *Lawrence Durrell: A Biography*, chapter 4.

Lawrence invited him to stay at Kalami, and during the summer of 1939, Henry Miller arrived.

It was then, while staying on a short visit to the Kalami house, that Lawrence introduced me to Henry Miller. I found him a very pleasant and amusing companion, a great talker and a man of extreme energy who never seemed to be able to keep still. In a curious way, he reminded me of many of the character traits of Lawrence himself although no two persons could have been more dissimilar in appearance. From the very first moment, Henry was a remarkable success with the local inhabitants; without knowing a word of Greek, he seemed to be able to understand them and make them understand *him*. Also he was very fond of clowning and had very humorous and mobile features with which he could send his audience into roars of laughter. He soon received the affectionate nickname of 'O Karaghiozis' after the principal comic hero of that name in the Greek shadow-show.

But Henry Miller also had another side to him, and that was a very live curiosity on every subject. Often, as we all sat under the night stars (I have written a poem on this subject),[43] on the sun-heated rocky plateau above the sea, he would ask me countless questions about astronomy. Later on in the same year, I was able to get an invitation for all three of us to the Athens Observatory, and I can still remember the excitement and enthusiasm of both Lawrence and Henry when, for the first time in their lives, they were able to see Saturn and his rings and the jewel-like Pleiades through the big telescope.[44] Henry Miller has written about all this in his book *The Colossus of Maroussi* (first published in 1941) in which I am one of the characters described – second only to Lawrence and George Katsimbalis, the Colossus himself.

---

[43] See the poem printed at the end of these memoirs, which Stephanides sent to Brigham in his letter containing corrections to the typescript, both of which are now held in the McPherson Library Special Collections at the University of Victoria.

[44] A further account of this visit to the Athens Observatory appears in the section 'In Athens' (below).

Henry Miller, like Lawrence, took a great delight in the Corfu wildflowers, especially the lovely pink cyclamen which had just begun to appear before he finally left the island. During my stay at Kalami, he was constantly bringing me flowers of every shape and colour and asking me their names. Apparently it came as a great surprise to him when he discovered that there were a good many specimens that I could *not* name.

One little episode comes to my mind. Owing, no doubt, to the rumours of war, it was almost impossible to find any more any foreign alcoholic drinks in Corfu. Lawrence and Henry often bemoaned the fact that gin (apparently one of the necessities of life) was practically unprocurable. One afternoon we three had gone for a walk on the main road above Kouloura and, on our way back, we stopped at a little wayside café to sample their brand of ouzo. But almost the first thing that caught Lawrence's eagle eye as we entered was a nearly full bottle of Gordon's Gin on a dusty shelf behind the counter. With the amazed look of a medieval knight who had just caught a glimpse of the Holy Grail, Lawrence pointed to it and, in a voice choked with emotion, asked the proprietor if it was for sale.

'Oh, that filthy stuff', answered the proprietor, 'you can have it and another five bottles I have in the cupboard. About twenty years ago I asked a cousin who was third mate on a small cargo boat that travelled between the Piraeus and Liverpool to bring me six bottles to try out here. But nobody here will drink it and, after one taste, I can't say that I blame them. You can have the lot at what they cost me and a good riddance – in fact I was thinking of throwing them away as they clutter up the place.'

'But how much will you want?' asked Lawrence breathlessly.

The proprietor gave a wink.

'Well, as my cousin saw to it that those bottles never passed through customs, I don't think the price will break you. You can have them for – drachmae each.' And he named a price which, at the then rate of exchange, worked out at about 5 shillings the bottle – 1939 shillings it is true. I saw a look come into Lawrence's and Henry's eyes as if they were Pizzaro's soldiers who had just stumbled upon an Inca horde of gold. And we departed each clutching two bottles of Gordon's Gin. There was jubilation in the Kalami home that evening. But, personally, I quite agree with the opinion of the café proprietor. Of all the horrid drinks I think that gin is about the horridest!

## Spyros the Chauffeur Drives Us to Palaeocastritsa

One fine afternoon in the late spring (probably May) of 1937, Spyros the Chauffeur turned up unexpectedly with his car at the Anemoyanni Villa. It must have been a Thursday, as Mary and I were spending the afternoon with the Durrell family. Lawrence and Nancy had also come over from Kalami.

Spyros suggested that, as it was such a fine day, he should drive us all to Palaeocastritsa to have tea at the Xenias Hotel. We all greeted the idea with alacrity except Margaret, who had washed her hair that morning, and Nancy, who was working against time in eliminating the spelling mistakes in one of Lawrence's typescripts. Leslie was not present, as he was running around after wild boar (or vice-versa) in Epirus and would not be back until supper time.

But the rest of us, old Mrs. Durrell, Mary, Lawrence, Gerald and I squeezed into the car with the anticipation of a very pleasant drive through the springtime landscape. Spyros' bulk occupied more than his fair share of the front seat, so the two least bulky members of our party, Mary and Gerald, sat beside him while the rest of us sat in the back of the car. At first all went swimmingly. Spyros was at his best, recounting all the latest gossip of the town in his bass voice and his special brand of Anglo-American speech. But just after we passed the branch road to the village of Skripero we saw in front of us a huge bus loaded to the gunnels with peasants and their numerous purchases after a morning's shopping in town.

The bus was trundling along at a sedate pace (rather strange for a Corfu bus!) raising a cloud of dust in which we were very soon enveloped. And, what was more, it was hugging the crown of the road so that there was no way of passing it as there was a steep bank on one side and a still steeper drop on the other.

Spyros sounded his horn until he nearly burst it, but it soon became evident that the driver of the bus had no intention of giving way to Spyros or to the devil himself. And thus we drove along in the dust for several miles, Spyros tooting his horn and yelling and getting madder and madder every moment. And what infuriated him still more (and us, too, for that matter) were the smiles and open jeers of the bus passengers who could look back and watch Spyros' discomfiture. The latter in the meanwhile was nearly breaking a blood vessel (or several blood vessels!):

'Him's Yannis from Lakones', he kept on repeating, 'I knows the bastards! Always having jokes, but I'll haves his ears for this! I'll shows him!'

Several times I expected him, in his fury, to ram the back of the bus, but he just managed to restrain himself.

Suddenly we were all jerked to the floor of the car in a confused struggling heap, and, before we could realise what was happening, our car had careered down a steep embankment and was bouncing and jouncing through an olive wood, Spyros twisting the wheel this way and that and avoiding rocks and tree trunks by fractions of an inch! Each time we tried to get up, we were thrown down again as the car bounced over some obstacle and, from their exclamations, we could tell that Mary and Gerald in the front seat were no happier than we were.

'The man's stark raving mad!' yelled Lawrence. 'Somebody ought to stop him before he kills us all!' But Spyros, with a grim set face, clung tenaciously to the wheel of the cavorting car and was deaf to all our expostulations. Suddenly we were all flung backwards by a still stronger jolt, the car seemed to be rearing up on its hind wheels as we rushed up a steep embankment, and then, to our great relief and amazement, there we were on the main road again, all in one piece and, what is more, *in front* of the bus instead of behind it. Then we understood Spyros' strategy. He had dashed down an embankment which was not quite steep enough to wreck the car, cut across a loop in the main road, climbed an embankment again and got ahead of the bus which had been obliged to follow the longer way around the curve. This manoeuvre had entailed driving the car at full tilt through an olive grove and nearly killing us all in the process, but these were secondary matters to Spyros when compared to besting 'the bastard from Lakones' or losing face in front of a whole bus load of spectators.

And, to tell the truth, after sorting ourselves out and finding that with the exception of a few scratches and bruises we had all miraculously escaped unhurt, we, too, rejoiced in Spyros' triumph. It had been very galling to trail along behind that bus and swallow its dust and know that the driver was having a game with us.

But now it was Spyros who was in front and who held the crown of the road. And he *crawled* along, with Yannis behind him so broken in spirit that he did not even once toot his horn. He knew that this would have been quite useless and that nothing would dislodge Spyros from the crown of the road or hurry his pace – it would have needed a shell from a twelve-inch gun to do so! 'I teacheds him, the bastards', observed Spyros gleefully, 'he's no goings to laughs at *me!*'

And so we crawled along, Spyros (and we also) savouring to the full our victory, until we reached the Lakones branch road where we continued left towards Palaeocastritsa and the bus turned right and was able to put on speed again. And so did we.

We had all completely recovered by the time we returned to the Anemoyanni Villa for supper through a scenery made fairy-like by thousands of flitting fire flies. But the story of our little adventure lost nothing in telling and I think that Nancy and Margaret were both rather relieved at having given the ride a miss. As for Leslie, his reaction was also characteristic: 'If I had been there with my boar gun, I would have blown the bastard Jannis into two bastards!'

## The Palatiano Villa

One day, in the winter or early spring of 1938 if I remember right, the Durrell family (with the exception, of course, of Lawrence and Nancy who remained at Kalami) moved from the Anemoyanni Villa at Sotiriotissa to the Palatiano Villa, a slightly smaller two-storied house. This was 'the Snow-White Villa' of Gerald's *My Family and Other Animals* and it was situated near the tiny village of Chrysida, about two kilometres south of Corfu Town as the crow flies, but a good deal longer by road. As before, Lawrence and Nancy would often stay here for a few days whenever they felt that they needed a change from Kalami.

As Lawrence said: 'You can have a little too much even of Paradise and a little taste of Hell every now and then is good for my work – keeps my brain from stagnating. You can trust Gerry to provide the Hell.' And if violent movement is good for the brain, Lawrence certainly got plenty of it, as our games of attacking and defending the castle were resumed with even more zest than before.

The grounds of the Palatiano Villa were even more rough and wooded than those of the villa at Sotiriotissa; cypress and olive trees were everywhere abundant, and the brushwood was so thick in some places as to form an almost impenetrable *maquis*. Not far from the house was a tiny white-washed stone chapel, and behind this was a small conical hillock that was eminently suitable for our games.

The presence of the chapel slightly favoured the attackers, as the building obstructed a section of the field of observation of the defenders of the knoll, and could be used as cover during an approach.

Lawrence was particularly adept at charging out from behind the chapel walls, and I can still remember the sight of him with his face red and his hair flapping about his forehead, his shirt pockets bulging with cypress cone ammunition and a cypress branch brandished in his good right hand. I can still hear his war cries as he charged up a slope, or his curses when he got entangled in the prickly undergrowth. We had even more strenuous battles than at the Villa Anemoyanni as the local gardener and man-of-all-work seemed to have at least half a dozen sons who were always conscripted (very willing conscripts they made) into our attacking and defending forces. As before, bruises and scratches (from the bushes) were a daily occurrence and the ladies of the party (except Margaret who often joined the fighting) complained that it cost them all their spare time just to repair the damage done to our clothes. But, looking back on those days, I think it was worth it.

The only fly in the ointment of that period that I can remember was a certain Captain James (surname forgotten) who lived in one of the smaller hotels in town and who seemed to make a point of turning up at tea-time far more often than any of us liked. He seemed, too, to have an uncanny knack of turning up whenever Lawrence and Nancy were in residence.

Captain James (he was a retired merchant Navy captain) was short, gnarled, red-faced, bald-headed and white-bearded.[45] He appeared to be in his nineties (very vigorous nineties), but was probably not quite as old as that. The reason for his unpopularity was that, from the first moment he appeared, he would monopolise the conversation. Neither Lawrence nor I were able to get in a word sideways. This would have been quite all right if any of his numerous anecdotes had been interesting. A man like him must surely have had plenty of thrilling adventures during his long life at sea that he could have told us. But instead of this, all his descriptions were only of the numerous landladies he had known all over the world and how they had all tried to overcharge him. 'Women are the same all over the world', was his usual refrain, 'always trying to get their claws into your last sixpence. Don't you agree with me, Mrs. Durrell?' Mrs. Durrell tactfully tried to gag him with another bun.

---

[45] This was almost certainly the model for 'Captain Patrick Creech', described graphically in Gerald Durrell's *Birds, Beasts and Relatives* (*The Corfu Trilogy*, pp. 506–20).

Captain James had a fine collection of oaths (which I could see Lawrence memorising for future literary needs) and he would bring these into the conversation in an innocent and off-hand manner as if he had long since forgotten their real meaning. He could also (much to Lawrence's chagrin) polish off anything drinkable in the house. Although, I must say, that I never saw him lose control of his faculties and he always departed under his own steam (sometimes it is true, rather unsteadily) whenever his instinct told him that there was not another bottle left in some hidden cupboard. I left Corfu for several months later on that summer and, when I returned in the late autumn, Captain James had left Corfu. I don't think any of us regretted him much.

I noticed, however, that even in the excitement of storming a fortress (whether at Sotiriotissa or at the Palatiano Villa) Lawrence always had his mind open for 'winged ideas' as he called them (or something very similar – it was something winged).

Sometimes in the middle of an attack he would suddenly dash off, amid protesting cries of 'Come back you \*\*\*!' from his own side and cheers from the other, to dash off to his room (where there was always paper and pencils ready for such emergencies) so as to get the idea down before it had been forgotten. Lawrence was always very conscientious about his work and never missed an opportunity of improving it. He never forgot that he intended and *was* going to be a great writer one day, and he kept that goal before him with great tenacity and confidence. And, such was his self-assurance, that we all took it for granted that he would manage it – anyway I did. But it did cost his side the victory on several occasions. I wonder if his mind ever rested when he looked relaxed and half asleep sunbathing on the Kalami rocks just above the sea.

# Lawrence Durrell
## and the Greek Shadow Play

Some time during the summer of 1936 or 1937, a Karaghiozis (Shadow-show) player came to Corfu. I think it was Theodorakis, a player from Patras, who often made the tour of the Ionian Islands, beginning at Corfu and ending up in Zante.[46]

He set up his 'theatre' in what was at that time a waste weed-overgrown flat place between the building of the one-time Ionian Academy (now a school) and the road running along the sea front to Garitsa Bay.[47] This 'theatre' consisted of about ten rows of rush-bottomed chairs and long wooden benches for the spectators, and a rough wooden shed with a long strip of white calico, about one yard high and seven or eight yards long, running across the front of it. This latter was the 'stage' on which the shadows of the puppets were projected, while the operators themselves remained hidden in the shed.

From the first moment, Lawrence (and to a lesser extent, Zarian) became fascinated with this sort of show and he has devoted a chapter to it in his book *Prospero's Cell*. The first time that Lawrence attended one of these shows, his knowledge of Greek was not yet very advanced (that is why I think it must have been as early as 1936), but the antics of the shadow-puppets and the folk-music that accompanied the performance

---

[46] When the Durrell School of Corfu presented Karaghiozis performances in Corfu in 2002, performed by puppet-master Evyenios Spatharis, it was believed that at least some of the performances witnessed by Durrell and Stephanides had been made by his father, Sotiris Spatharis. Durrell mentions in *Prospero's Cell* that some performances took place in the garden of the Italian School (location unknown to the editors). Stephanides himself undertook extensive research on the subject of Karaghiozis, with the intention of collaborating with Durrell on a separate book, but this did not materialise. His material is located in the Durrell archive at Southern Illinois University, Carbondale.

[47] This area is the south tip of the Esplanade in Corfu Town, across the street from the Ionian Academy and the Cavalieri Hotel.

were an entertainment in themselves.

After the show, Lawrence, Nancy, Gerald and I (as interpreter) went into the shed and introduced ourselves to the proprietor. The latter, very politely, showed us the various puppets made of flat pieces of jointed cardboard, sometimes with inlays of coloured transparent materials. These were placed flat against the calico screen and very cleverly mani-pulated on the end of one or two long thin rods. The light came, of course, from behind the manipulator and thus, from in front, the puppets appeared as sharp edged, dark shadows on a brightly illuminated white background.

The proprietor (Theodorakis?), a man of between 40 and 50 years, was helped by two younger men, perhaps his sons, but it was he who imitated most of the different voices and accents and did most of the difficult bits. His dexterity was astonishing and he sometimes manipulated two puppets at the same time. Lawrence, and the rest of us, all tried our hands at manipulating these puppets. But we very soon discovered that this was not for us, and that many years of practice would be necessary to become even moderately proficient. In fact Theodorakis affirmed that one had to be born and brought up in a 'Karaghiozis family' to be able to become a good 'Karaghiozis player'. And I for one believe that he was very probably right.

Several times after that occasion, Karaghiozis shows were given in Corfu town and, occasionally, at the village of Kassiopi, not far from Kalami, and Lawrence always tried to be present whenever he could spare the time from his literary work.

# Paper Games, Corfu

During the long (and often cold and wet) winter evenings of 1936 and 1937 when Lawrence and Nancy would often come to stay for a few days with the rest of the Durrell family at the Anemoyanni Villa at Sotiriotissa, we would spend very pleasant hours with a big fire of fragrant cypress and olive wood burning in the living room fire-place – the only fire-place that the villa possessed (like most Corfu houses, it relied on stoves or braziers for winter heating).

Sometimes, as mentioned previously, I would bring gramophone records of Greek folk dances in which we all joined and worked up a splendid appetite for supper in the process. At other times, especially after supper, we would gather round a big table and indulge in various table games. I can't remember that we played any card games, but *Halma* was not unpopular. But what we liked best was various writing games at which we were all fairly good and at which Lawrence, naturally, excelled.

One of these was the ancient and well-known 'Consequences', in the course of which we libelled most of our friends and acquaintances and most of the world's celebrities, alive and dead. In fact some of the results were so exceedingly libellous that old Mrs. Durrell considered it one of her chores to gather up all the sheets of paper after every session and throw them on the fire.

Another game, however, was even more popular, as it left much more scope and initiative to the literary imagination. This game, 'Best Sellers', was introduced by Lawrence – I don't know if he had invented it himself or not. The rules were simple. Before the game, we would decide on the names of the hero, the heroine, the villain, and any other characters who might, in our opinion, come in useful for the story. Then each player in turn would write six lines of a story and fold the sheet of paper so as to leave only the *last* line visible. The next player would have to continue from what he had gathered by this last line, and so on round and round the circle until the story was judged complete. It was usually left to Lawrence to round off the tale by writing the last six lines and then to read us out the whole story. This would usually be quite a difficult feat for even Lawrence to accomplish, for the *non sequiturs* were often so funny that both he and the rest of us would be in a continuous roar of laughter. I kept a lot of these results, which would still have made very amusing reading, but, unfortunately, they were lost together with much else, when my brother-in-law's flat was bombed during World War II.

This was a game in which we all joined, even old Mrs. Durrell when we could persuade her to leave her housework. Lawrence was, of course, the star performer; but Gerald already showed a lot of promise. And I think that I was quite good at it also – although I say so myself. Curious to say, many years later, in 1941, during the Cretan Campaign, I introduced 'Best Sellers' to some of the other officers. Again with success, as I have described in my book *Climax in Crete*.

Less often, we would play another not too dissimilar paper-game which we called, if I remember right, 'Chimeras' or something similar. In this game, the first player would start a *drawing* of a human being or an animal, beginning by the head. He would then fold over the paper leaving only the *neck* visible and pass it on to the next player, without telling him what was the head he had drawn. The next player would complete the animal (or man) down to the waist or middle, and the third player would complete the hind or lower feet. In this game several pictures were started simultaneously as only three players were needed to complete each paper. Here, too, many very amusing results were achieved; but this game could not vie with 'Best Seller' in general popularity.

Incidentally, I tried to introduce chess – without much success. Lawrence declared that it was more like work than a relaxation and that if he had to work, then he preferred to work at something of literary value. No doubt he was right.

I mentioned previously that the sitting-room fire-place was the only one in the house. This was, perhaps, lucky, as the

Corfu builder did not seem at his best when building fire-places. One winter night, while staying at Sotiriotissa, Lawrence woke up in the small hours, coughing and sneezing, to find that the bedroom was full of smoke. He rushed downstairs, encountering more smoke, and found that the wooden floor around the sitting-room fire-place was charred and smouldering. Lawrence immediately raised the alarm and he and Leslie put out the threatening conflagration with a few buckets of water.

Afterwards, when workmen were called in for repairs, it was found that the wooden floorboards continued on *under the fireplace* – a rather strange manner of building a fireplace.

The Durrells, when retiring to bed, had left a half burnt log on the fire and this had caused the accident. The floorboards beneath the fireplace had probably been charring for weeks without anybody knowing, and it was very lucky that the whole house had not been burnt down that night. In fact it was strange that the fire had not happened earlier.[48]

---

[48] A bizarre version of this incident is to be found in Gerald Durrell's *My Family and Other Animals* (*Corfu Trilogy*, pp. 192–4).

# Some Victorian Relics

In 1935 and until the outbreak of World War II, Corfu was still well off the usual tourist track and in some of the older shops and cafés one still came across unexpected survivals from late and even middle Victorian times. These relics delighted Lawrence Durrell who often bemoaned the fact that his ready funds did not enable him to buy up quite a lot of old pieces of furniture and other odds and ends that he would come across.

Even as it was, the sitting-room of the Kalami house did contain a few pieces of Victorian bric-à-brac, old chemist jars with their Latin names, hair pin dishes, and so on that Nancy always dusted herself with great care. The walls also displayed a few similar 'finds' – the only one of which I can remember now was an advertisement for 'Rowlands Macassar Oil for the Hair' showing a young woman with luxuriant tresses reaching almost to the ground.

Lawrence claimed that his ambition was to obtain the sign over an old café just by the port. This depicted an enormous and ferocious-looking black cat and below it (in English) the words 'Black Cat Bar'. From the look of this sign, it might well have been originally painted in the middle of the last century and had only been repainted and touched up from time to time. Lawrence thought that it would look very well as a wall decoration above the mantlepiece. But he admitted that it was, perhaps, a little too big. This I can well imagine as, judging by memory, this sign must have been about 15 ft x 4 ft. Sad to say, when I visited Corfu again in 1961 this old sign had gone (although the bar had retained its old name)[49] and had been replaced by a miserable modern outrage. I didn't bother to enquire if the old sign had been destroyed during

---

[49] The Mavro Gato bar and restaurant, established in the nineteenth century, is still active on the ground floor of the Konstantinoupolis Hotel in Corfu Town, facing into the Old Port under the New Fortress.

the bombing or had been the victim of modernisation. The former end is very probable, as that quarter of the town had suffered very heavily.

# IN ATHENS – EARLY DAYS OF WORLD WAR II

About May 1938 I left Corfu for several months to work on the anti-malaria campaign in Macedonia with the Rockefeller Institute which had a big anti-malaria laboratory in Salonica under the direction of Dr. Balfour. Consequently I was able to see the Durrells much less frequently and only at long intervals until the summer of 1939 when Henry Miller arrived in Corfu.

When World War II broke out, 1st September 1939, Lawrence and Nancy Durrell happened to be in Athens, or arrived there very soon after that date, where they installed themselves in a very pleasant little fourth-floor flat in Anagnostopoulou Street, n° 40, very near the fashionable Kolonaki Square. Henry Miller was also in Athens at the same time and stayed there for several weeks before departing for America. It was during this period that Lawrence and Henry saw a lot of George Katsimbalis and went for several motor car trips with him in the Peloponnese, as described in Miller's book *The Colossus of Maroussi*.

At the very outbreak of the war, the British Embassy in Athens found itself very short of staff before further members could be sent out to them from England. People who could speak both English and Greek were then at rather a premium, and Lawrence Durrell and I were both taken on as part of an emergency temporary staff.

My own duties were simple and not very exciting. Every morning when I arrived at the office, situated on the ground floor of a house near the Embassy, I would find a big pile of Greek newspapers with some of their contents marked with a red pencil. These articles I had to translate into English and that, apart from translating an occasional letter (mostly from tradesmen and shopkeepers who dealt with the Embassy), was about all that was required of me. Not very glamorous – but I suppose that I was of some use. Anyway, I hoped that I was.

Lawrence Durrell's job was a bit more interesting. The German Embassy circulated a kind of official bulletin giving, naturally, the German point of view about everything. The British Embassy therefore decided to publish its own news bulletin as a counterweight. Lawrence, together with several others, produced this bulletin and even printed it, too, on a kind of mimeograph machine kept in the basement. It looked rather strenuous work, as a large number of copies had to be run off in a very limited time, and Lawrence could generally be found running around with great quantities of sheets of damp paper which were hung up on clothes lines to dry so that the whole place was always festooned with them. Nancy had also quite a lot of homework to do, helping to edit these bulletins; but she did not go out much, as, at that time, she was expecting her first baby. I do not know what effect this bulletin had on the war, but I should think that it was by no means a waste of time, as it was in great demand and all the copies printed were soon snapped up. However, we did not enjoy our glory as temporary officials of the Embassy for very long as, in about a month, the extra staff needed arrived from England and all the temporary wallahs were thrown out on their ears.

It was during this period, about the beginning of October if I remember right, that I was able to get permission to bring Lawrence and Henry to see the Athens Astronomical Observatory. One of the astronomers working there was John Phocas, whom I had known well in Corfu, and he very kindly piloted us round and showed us the sights. I cannot now remember if the moon was visible on that night, but we were shown the Pleiades and Saturn with his rings through the big telescope. It was a memorable night for us all and Henry Miller has recorded it in *The Colossus of Maroussi*.

Soon after this date we all separated again, Henry Miller to return to America, Lawrence Durrell to remain in Athens working for the British Council, and I to return to Corfu to await my call-up for the Royal Army Medical Corps which arrived in June 1940. Before leaving for Corfu, I met the other members of the Durrell family in Athens for just one morning. They were on their way to catch the steamer at Piraeus that would take them back to England. I can't remember if this was slightly before or after the declaration of war.⁵⁰ My orders were to report to the Army Medical Authorities in Cyprus. This meant that I would have to go overland via Athens, Constantinople, Ankara and Beirut, as, owing to Mussolini's threats to sink neutral shipping, no ships were running between Greece and Cyprus.

I arrived in Athens on 11 June 1940 and saw the Durrells who were staying at the same flat in Anagnostopoulou Street. Since I last saw them, Penelope had been born – a fine and lusty baby of a few weeks old. I left Athens again on the first leg of my journey to Cyprus on 18 June and did not see the Durrells again until I met them in Egypt after the fall of Crete.

---

⁵⁰ Lawrence and Nancy left Corfu in early September 1939, immediately upon the declaration of war; the rest of the family had already returned to England in June, in anticipation of hostilities.

# In Egypt after the Fall of Crete

After I had been evacuated from Crete, on board H.M.A.S. 'Perth', I arrived at Alexandria on 1 June 1941 and was immediately sent on to Cairo (I was then a Lieutenant in the R.A.M.C.) that same night – in the midst of an air raid – and told to report to the R.A.M.C. Base Depot in that town. I put up at the Carlton Hotel where, by good luck, I met David Abercrombie whom I had already met in Athens where he worked for the British Council.[51]

It was from Abercrombie that I learnt of Lawrence and Nancy's whereabouts – they were staying temporarily at the Luna Park Hotel, a rather ramshackle place that the authorities had requisitioned to house British refugees from German-invaded Europe. After the usual delays and wrong numbers, I had the pleasure of hearing Lawrence's voice on the phone and had the pleasure of going round and seeing him again that same afternoon. The Luna Park Hotel was a terrible place and terrifically overcrowded, but Lawrence and Nancy and baby Penelope looked very well, considering what they had been through.

I learnt from Lawrence that he had been working at the British Council School at Kalamata in the southern Peloponnese, and had managed to get away in a small *caïque* crowded with other refugees, just one day before the entry of the Germans. They had spent several very uncomfortable and dangerous days at sea, expecting at any moment to be attacked by German or Italian planes and knowing well that, in its overcrowded state, the *caïque* would founder if even a moderate storm arose.

---

[51] Ian MacNiven (*Lawrence Durrell: A Biography*, pp. 234–5) records that Abercrombie 'sent Stephanides to Larry. Theodore was limping after having walked across Crete in borrowed boots several sizes too large... Theodore told Larry that all who had been part of the evacuation from Crete would receive a medal "inscribed with the words EX CRETA".' Abercrombie was the son of poet Lascelles Abercrombie.

But their luck held, and they arrived safely in Alexandria where they thought that their troubles were at last over. But things did not turn out quite so pleasantly. The moment they set foot ashore, all the occupants of the *caïque*,[52] including the Durrells, were pounced on by the military authorities and interned in a concentration camp where they were even more overcrowded than in the Luna Park Hotel. This was done routinely as a precaution to prevent German agents from being smuggled into Egypt together with the genuine refugees.

The Durrells, fortunately, were able to prove their *bona fides* after a short delay, but then another difficulty presented itself. They had escaped from Kalamata with only what they stood up in and this did not include any cash. This is why they had resided, as guests of the authorities, at the unprepossessing Luna Park Hotel. But this, too, had now been overcome. Funds had been telegraphed to them and they were already due to leave for the Gezira Guest House as soon as the flat they had taken there was ready for them – a matter of another day or two.

By good luck, I was given a temporary posting to the 15th (Scottish) General Hospital at Agusa, a pleasant suburb of Cairo on the bank of the Nile. By even better luck, this hospital was only a short walk from the Gezira Guest House, a very pleasant block of flats in the middle of the exclusive Gezira Island between two branches of the Nile. It was on this island that most of the British officials, both military and civil, lived with their families.

My work as Assistant Radiologist was not too onerous and I was soon able to visit the Durrells at their new flat, which Nancy had made quite home-like and comfortable – in spite of the fact that Lawrence insisted that all *he* required was a bed, a mosquito-net and a typewriter. I cannot remember if a table and chair were included in this list. Perhaps not, as I have seen

---

[52] This is not strictly accurate, as the *caïque* in which the Durrells had escaped from Kalamata had put in at Chania, in Crete, and they had transferred to an Australian troop ship for the journey to Alexandria.

Lawrence at Kalami tapping away quite happily at his typewriter while sitting on a flat beach with the typewriter between his knees.

Lawrence soon obtained an important post on the staff of the Intelligence Department's Information Office, where his writing ability and his knowledge of Greek and French were at a great premium. In spite of his exacting work at the Information Office, Lawrence still managed to devote a part of his life to literature, together with a number of other writers, both English and Greek, most of whom, male and female, I was introduced to at one time or another. But it is so long ago that I have forgotten most of their names. He founded a monthly journal [*Personal Landscape*] which continued to appear until the end of the war. Many of the contributors to this journal, besides Lawrence Durrell himself, have since become famous in literature; one of them was George Seferiades (George Seferis) who won the Nobel Prize for Literature in 1968. I only wish that I could quote the names of some of the other authors, but all my numbers of *Personal Landscape* were lost, together with most of my kit, during the many displacements of the Western Desert War, and this is why I can't refresh my memory by looking them up.[53]

Sometimes I would meet Lawrence and Nancy (when she was not too occupied with Penelope) during the evenings at the Gezira Club — I believe its official title was the Mohammed Ali Club, but my memory may be wrong. Here we would often gather round a table with some of the other writers and discuss literature for hours. Most of this conversation was a bit over my head, but I think that I *looked* as if I understood it all. At one time Lawrence also undertook to teach me billiards, but

---

[53] *Personal Landscape* was edited by Durrell, Robin Fedden and Bernard Spencer, with Terence Tiller as adviser. Other contributors included G.S. Fraser, Olivia Manning, Keith Douglas, Dorian Cooke and Gwyn Williams: cf. Jonathan Bolton, *Personal Landscapes: British Poets in Egypt During the Second World War* (New York: St. Martin's Press, 1997) and Roger Bowen, *"Many Histories Deep": the* Personal Landscape *Poets in Egypt, 1940–45* (London: Associated University Presses, 1995).

without any success. Incidentally, I never learnt if Lawrence actually *knew* how to play billiards, but this was no obstacle to his *teaching* someone how to play.

Lawrence was always a good mixer, and soon got to know anybody worth knowing, so I was not surprised when he told me that Professor Reisner[54] had invited us both to have tea with him at his camp near the Pyramids and would himself show us one of the Queen's Tombs.

Professor Reisner was a famous American Egyptologist who had done a great deal of excavation work on many ancient Egyptian sites. Lawrence and I had a very pleasant tea under a big white marquee served by waiters in white flowing robes and red sashes. The camp looked quite a luxurious place – though Professor Reisner assured us that archaeological work was not always quite so comfortable.

After tea, the Professor took us round to one of the tiny pyramids which surround the three great ones. It was in these tiny pyramids that the mummies of the royal wives were buried. After descending a dark sloping passage, lit by a big electric battery lamp which one of the professor's servants carried, we reached a fairly large stone chamber with a stone sarcophagus on a pedestal in the centre. The sarcophagus was empty, as the mummy of Queen (name forgotten) had been removed to the Cairo Museum.[55] The professor told us her history and the date when her tomb had been excavated, and showed and explained to us what I thought was the most interesting item of the tomb.

This was a continuous dado of small brightly coloured pictures which went all round the room and which showed scenes from the daily life of the Egypt of that period. These *paintings* were made in great detail and in colours, which, owing to their having been always in darkness, had not faded from the

---

[54] George Andrew Reisner (1867–1942) was a major Egyptologist who discovered the tomb of Queen Hetepheres I. He was nearly blind by this time, and he died the year after this tour.

[55] This very likely refers to Queen Hetepheres I, though the mummy is lost, and the contents of the tomb are in the Cairo Museum.

day they had been painted. Reisner remarked that workmen were (and are) the same in all countries and in all ages, and showed us that where the paintings had been partly hidden (by furniture now removed) the painters had skimped their work and the drawings were far less carefully executed. But, on the whole, they were beautifully done and one could see fishermen on the Nile, weavers at their looms, potters at their wheels, housewives at their housework and all the other scenes of a busy world.

Professor Reisner also showed us another curious fact. On one of the walls of the funeral chamber there was a square fairly deep niche, containing the small bust of a man. This niche had been bricked in and concealed in Egyptian times and had only been discovered during the excavation works. This bust was *not* that of the Queen's husband, and it was conjectured that it had been smuggled into its place, perhaps by a lover with some religious idea of the two being joined again after death.

This excursion took place, if I remember right, some time in September 1941. Not long afterwards, in November 1941, I was posted away from Cairo to n° 58 General Hospital at Amiriya near Alexandria, and so my pleasant meetings with Lawrence ended until 28 February 1942, when I was given a week's leave for Cairo and so had the pleasure of seeing Lawrence again. My leave had come at very short notice and I had some difficulty in finding a hotel room in overcrowded Cairo, but Lawrence came to my rescue with another of his interesting friends. He introduced me to Christopher Buckley, the war correspondent to the *Daily Telegraph*, who had a flat on Gezira Island very near the Durrells. Christopher Buckley very kindly put me up for my short stay and so I was able to spend most of my time with Lawrence when *he* had any spare time. This was not always easy, as he was up to his ears with his work in the Information Department and his frequent contributions to *Personal Landscape*. Besides which he was already taking copious notes of the new life around him for future use. And probably he was already shaping in his mind the outlines of the novels which were later on to become famous as his

*Alexandria Quartet.*

After that week in Cairo, the hectic period of the Rommel battles took place. 58 General Hospital retreated hurriedly from Mersa Matruk in the Western Desert to Moascar on the Suez Canal, near Ismailia. After Rommel had been held on the El Alamein Line, a period of relative calm set in and, on 14 August 1942, I was able to get a week-end leave for Cairo and meet Lawrence Durrell again.

I found him brisk, cheerful and optimistic in spite of the recent flap. As before, he was still working (or rather overworking) in the Information Department, and was so well considered by his superiors that he was soon to be made Director of the Alexandria Branch of the Information Department. When I now saw him, Lawrence was living alone, as Nancy and little Penelope had been hurriedly shipped off to Beirut during the evacuation of British families at the time of the Rommel advance.

At about this time a fairly regular military bus service was run between Ismailia and Cairo and I was able to see Lawrence again on 6 and 26 September, always looking fit and brimful of energy.

Soon after this, however, Lawrence was transferred to Alexandria as head of the Alexandrian branch of the Intelligence and Information Department with an office and staff of his own. I was not able to see him again until 15 January 1943, when I stayed for a fortnight in Alexandria while 58 General Hospital was getting ready to move to Bengazi, which had been evacuated in the meanwhile by Rommel's forces after his defeat by Montgomery at El Alamein. Lawrence was in his element; he was now his own boss and he was able to make good use of his knowledge of Greek as, at that time, Alexandria still contained a numerous Greek population. I visited him several times at his office, a busy place with the walls well covered with anti-German political posters in several languages.

It was nearly ten months before we again had an opportunity of meeting, as 58 General Hospital first went to

Bengazi, then Tripoli and from there to Sicily during the campaigns which drove the Germans out of that island. Towards the middle of October 1943 I found myself back in Alexandria, where I had been evacuated with a bad attack of dysentery and enterocolitis and, while a patient in 64 General Hospital, I had the pleasure of a visit from Lawrence Durrell who was still working in his Alexandrian office.

On 19 December 1943, I was given a fortnight's sick-leave which I spent with Lawrence at the very pleasant house he shared with Mr. and Mrs. Paul Gotch[56] (who worked in the British Council), at 12 Rue Maamoun in one of the pleasantest quarters of Alexandria, composed mostly of detached villas surrounded by flowering gardens.[57] It was here that I spent one of the nicest Christmases I had ever enjoyed. By this time, Lawrence knew all about Alexandria, and he showed me the sites of some of its ancient monuments, including that of the Library and the famous Pharos. It was very interesting to look at the places where these famous monuments had once been, but, alas!, no ruins even of them still existed.

One of our favourite walks, when Lawrence could spare the time from his work, was the long promenade along the sea front [the Corniche] with the Mediterranean on one side and the long line of low clustered villas on the other. The weather, fortunately, was on the whole fine; but an icy north wind sometimes blew accompanied by sudden showers of rain. The Alexandria beach was studded with a number of small beach houses; some of them, however, were quite large and elaborate – almost as big as small villas with two, three or four rooms.

On several occasions I was rather surprised to see

---

[56] Durrell wrote the Introduction to Paul Gotch's *Three Caravan Cities* (Alexandria: Whitehead, 1945), and the two seem to have remained in contact for some time.

[57] This mansion, in fact at no. 17 (now 19) rue Maamoun, in the Moharrem Bey area, was owned by the Jewish family of Ambron, by whose name it is commonly called; after Nancy Durrell's departure, Lawrence was living there with his future second wife, Eve; in the garden of the mansion was a studio occupied by the painter Clea Badaro.

furniture standing out in the rain, until Lawrence explained to me that these beach houses belonged to the Alexandria Municipality which rented them out. If the rent was not paid up promptly, the lessee's furniture (the houses were let unfurnished) was just thrown out and the house rented to someone else, as there was always a big demand for them. Lawrence added that clerical errors were frequent and that you sometimes found your furniture thrown out even though you *had* paid your rent in time. Sometimes the same house was rented to two different people at once – with considerable dissatisfaction all round.

On 11 July 1944, I obtained another fortnight's leave, this time from Barce in Libya, and again spent another very pleasant holiday with Lawrence and the Gotches at their Alexandrian home. As before, Lawrence was still head of the Alexandria branch of the Information Office and up to his eyebrows in work – on which, however, he seemed to thrive.

Before the end of 1944, in September, I was transferred to 53 General Hospital with destination Salonica. But we first spent six weeks at Aba-el-Kader, just outside Alexandria, before we finally left Egypt in the first week of November. During that period, owing to a good (military) bus service, I was able to visit Lawrence on many occasions (mostly on a Saturday) and it was on one of these Saturday afternoons that he first introduced me to a charming young girl, Eve, who soon became his second wife and, later on, the mother of his second daughter, Sappho.

# FROM STEPHANIDES' CORRESPONDENCE

In his correspondence with James Brigham, Theodore Stephanides mentions 'a Larry Durrell anecdote which may amuse you': 'Larry mentioned that both he & Gerry are often presented with each other's books & requested to sign them. "On these occasions", Larry said, "we both use the same formula: 'In the absence of the *real* author of this book, it is hereby signed by a still better author'; this is followed by our own signature." Larry added that "One day a lady brought me a copy of *My Family and Other Animals* to sign. After she had read what I had written, she turned to me with a look of immense surprise & the words 'What! Do *you* also write books like your brother?'"'

In 1961, on a visit to his daughter and son-in-law, Theodore wrote to Lawrence Durrell:

> 'It may interest you to know that you are a terrific celebrity here in Athens & I am basking in quite a nimbus of reflected glory as "the Man who knows Lawrence Durrell!" This is how I am generally introduced to others, & I have kept whole audiences rapt with my Durrell anecdotes. The favourite seems to be the one where you were captured in King Faruk's harem, but got away with it by saying that you had come to read the gas meter & promising to knock 40,000 cubic feet off the Palace bill. Close second is the one where you stole a camel & rode through the streets of Cairo in your pajamas waving a purple banner with the slogan "Drink Coka-kola & down with the Bourgeoisie!"'

His correspondence with James Brigham ends with the following 'Corfu Poem', originally published in his *Cities of the Mind* (1969), 'which describes an evening enjoyed by Larry, Henry Miller and myself at Kalami, in August 1939':

## Corfu Poem

We sat beneath the silent stars of heaven
Upon a rock the sun had scorched all day,
And felt within us and around the leaven
Of Night's reprieve to Life. Below us lay
A blackness where the wavelets stirred and rippled,
Unseen, along a darkened beach; but soon,
Lit by a brightening sky, their crests were stippled
With silver spores sown by a rising moon
Until the quickened sea became a flowering
Of living quivering silver.
                        Then the night
Thrilled us once more with awe for, from a grove
Of cypresses that crowned the headland towering
Across the bay, a shepherd's piping wove
A tune of high thin threads of shivering light.

# Autumn Gleanings

## AURORA BOREALIS
(seen from Corfu, 24th March 1940)

The day was ended, but the northern sky
Shone with an angry red. Its crimson light
Turned the remembered beauty of the night
Into an alien splendour that the eye
Saw with both fear and wonder. In that red
The sweet familiar stars seemed shrunk and pale
(But faded ghosts of light) and some had fled,
Their beams extinguished by that shimmering veil
That welled, encroaching, up the sky. Below
A mountain pinnacle upreared its head,
A wedge of black against a scarlet bow.

The Heavens flamed a presage in that glow,
Reflections of the tides that were to flow
Red and more red ere that dread Year was dead.[58]


## DISTANT THUNDERSTORM AT NIGHT

The lightning twists across the skies
In writhings like a dying snake;
Its flicker beats upon my eyes
And keeps me wide awake.
I wince with each contorted flash,
But every time the clouds stay dumb;
I listen for that thunder-crash
That never seems to come!

---

[58] On 28 October 1940 (known in Greece as 'Ochi Day') the Greek government rejected Mussolini's demand that Greece should open its borders to the Italian army, and the Italian army attempted to invade Greece from the Albanian border. The invasion was successfully repulsed, but led to the decisive entry of German troops into Greece in April 1941.

## SUNSET

As night approaches, for awhile the sky
Takes on a vivid glory that before
This hour was uncreated. Now the eye
Is held entranced by rippling hues that soar
From cloud to clustered cloud like swirls and waves
Upon a windy, world-encircling sea…
An ocean of concordant tones… octaves
Of coloured fire instead of melody.

I gaze and wonder: what is this that fills
My being and can sway me by its might?
What is this thing in me that joys and thrills
To frequencies and wave-lengths of mere light?
What is this mystery, and can its spark
Be chilled for ever by encroaching dark?


## THE UNIVERSE

I shall be dead one day and all I know:
The knowledge that I gathered down the years,
The memories of loves and joys and tears,
Will all these vanish like a flake of snow
Touched by the springtime sun? It may be so;
Perhaps this universe is meaningless,
A mocking jest, an empty sham, a mess…
Then may I close my eyes and bid it go.

## INSOMNIA

With old age I have come to hate the night,
For, owing to the glow of London's skies,
I cannot see the stars, once my delight,
That soothed me until slumber closed my eyes.
In that past time the hours knew shorter flight
Before sleep sought the couch on which I lay;
Light were my dreams, and soon the morning light
Aroused me gently to a newer day.
But now the dark seems endless… When I look
For comfort to the stars, they are not there –
The skies show only that accursed red glare!

Then I take from the shelf another book
On which I can no longer concentrate…
Till once more I turn off the lamp… and wait…


## QUESTION

I often feel that I would like to wake
All Life to Love – not only beings we clothe
In graceful forms, but also those that take
The hideous semblances we shun and loathe.
We shudder at the writhing parasite,
Yet it did not demand or choose its shape;
Why was it then cast out into the night
And shackled to a fate of no escape?

## ICE AGE

The Last Man gazed at the frosty sky
And the chill air piped in his labouring lungs,
While the sunbeams glimmered in tremulous rungs
On his upturned face as he lay down to die...

Cold, cold spun upon the Earth, an ice-bound plain,
Estranged alike from deep-flowing main
And from sky-soaring mountain;
For by wind, rain and fountain,
The peak to the steppe had been levelled again.
And the oceans had dwindled to deserts of mud,
Each draining the Earth of her life and her blood,
Till the children she'd suckled so long at her breast
Had cursed her and perished.

                        From East now to West,
And from North on to South to their ultimate zones
Lay spread a white shroud, and two crystalline thrones
Loomed vast and unreal in that wan waste of snow.
And the sun, as it sank to its low twilight gate,
Cast the last blood-red beam of its desolate glow
On two mighty Forms sitting silent in state:
The two awesome Angels of Death and of Cold.

And they brooded alone... while the Earth, which of old
Had thrilled to past glories of Mind and of Lyre,
Of Love and of Beauty, of Hope and of Fire,
Sped silent and soulless – the Song of the Spheres
A gibe at her sorrow, a mock at her tears.

## TERMITE COSMOLOGIST

A Termite said: "We must be up to date,
Abandon superstition, myth, and dream;
Abjure those shams whose mind-corroding spate
Has borne us overlong upon its stream.

"There is no Man whom we were taught to see
Rewarding Virtue with a glut of wood;
Or belching clouds of deadly D.D.T.
When Evil dared to raise its serpent hood.

"There is no Man. He did not make this chair
Into whose tasty depths our tunnels wind;
It made itself from empty air
By random particles that spun and twined.

"Those casual particles, for time untold,
Danced aimlessly like gnats in summer glade;
They jittered, jostled, rioted and rolled,
Till slowly, just by chance, this chair was made.

"Who made these random particles and why?
Why do they, why does *anything* exist?
I'll think that up and answer by and by –
But Man, meanwhile, has vanished into mist!"

# FIVE QUATRAINS

*Eclipse*
The sun is by the moon eclipsed – a sight
To prove that in the sky, as here below,
The lesser may the greater overthrow,
And splendour may be overcome by night!

*Air waves*
A spiral groove upon a disk
Is all the eye can see;
But in that time the subtler ear
Thrills to a melody!

*Homo superior*
Man's superiority is plain to see:
He is more handsome than the chimpanzee;
But would he pass a beauty test so well
If pitted against peacock or gazelle?!

*The goad*
The thing of things that did the most to shape
Man's brain and raise him higher than the ape
Was just his urge to poke and pry and see –
In short: his apish curiosity.

*Skylark*
A speck that soars till lost to sight,
A cadence from the skies
That seems to crystallise
The quintessence of light.

## HAIL ON A TIN ROOF

A steady drumming rises to a roar,
Or falls to a few isolated taps.
These coalesce again as the downpour
Becomes so heavy that the single raps
Of hailstones blend into a wild tattoo,
A roll, a racket, a hullabaloo,
A din, the devil drum-alarm from hell –
Then sudden silence louder than a yell!


## CHRISTMAS AFTERMATH

They decked my boughs with toys and coloured lights,
And danced around me. For a few short days
I was the centre of a world's delights,
The focus of its plaudits and its praise.

Then of a sudden, I have not learnt why,
I was degraded by a dark decree;
And in the dustbin here, despised, I lie,
A withered and discarded Christmas Tree.

# CELESTIAL PARADOX

We do not see the stars by night
(Or even their refracted ghosts)
As one array; those shining hosts
Form no coherent scheme of light.

Bright Sirius to us appears
By beams it launched *nine* years ago;
Yet to the past *eleven* years
We venture with Procyon's glow.

Full *twenty-seven* years the gleam
Of Vega took to reach our eyes;
For Rigel's rays to cross the skies
*Nine plodding centuries* did stream.

Thus, when towards the stars we gaze,
A sky that never was we see;
A vast, confused, entangled maze
Where Space and Time blend mockingly![59]

---

[59] Sirius, known colloquially as the 'Dog Star' (*Canis major*), is the brightest star in the night sky, due both to its intrinsic luminosity and to its closeness to the Sun; Procyon is the brightest star in the constellation *Canis minor* and forms one of the three vertices of the 'Winter Triangle' with Sirius and Betelgeuse; Vega is a relatively nearby star, and the fifth brightest, which has been termed 'arguably the next most important star in the sky after the Sun'; Rigel is the sixth brightest star, the most luminous in the Milky Way, and measurements of its distance from Earth vary between seven and nine hundred light-years.

## FIRST GREETING

When sons of Earth and Mars[60] first meet in space
And on some asteroid stand face to face,
The one: "It has no mouth, this Martian freak!"
The other: "Earthly brute, it has no beak!"

And then? It may be difficult to read
A Martian's mind; but as for our own breed,
To guess *his* thought should not require much skill:
"When this Thing turns its back, I'll shoot to kill!"

## GOLDEN LYRE

Amid the embers of the dying fire
Bright pictures form and fade. Beyond the grate,
 I see the semblance of a golden lyre
Whose strings of amber glitter and pulsate;
And with each pulse a spire of silver smoke
Climbs thinly upwards like a cypress-tree…
That lyre is ash, but still it can evoke
An evanescent spark of melody.

---

[60] 'Or any other planet': TS's footnote.

## MISCALCULATION

When I was young, time lagged so slow
I often tried to spur the hours;
I longed to feel brave Summer suns,
Spring seemed insipid with her flowers.

I must have pressed those hours so hard
That they outraced the years, else how
Can I explain this overleap:
For here I walk with Winter now!


## LONDON UNDER SNOW

All night it snowed and, when the morning came,
All London lay beneath a quilt of light;
Each blemish had been veiled, each blot and shame
Had been redeemed, smoothed over, and made right.
But soon on every street the snowflakes bright
In greasy heaps of mud and slush were piled;
On hedge and lawn the snow still glimmered white –
Only where Man had trod was it defiled.

## LONDON PLANE (*Platanus acerifolia* Wildenow)[61]

I once was sired by East and West,
But here in London I thrive best;
For, with my bark, from day to day
All smuts, like sins, are shed away;
And London's drizzle washes clear
My smooth green leaves of soot and smear.
Old Oxford knew me first of all
And then in London I grew tall,
And ever I extend my gains
Across this "City of the Planes".

---

[61] The *Platanus acerifolia* Wildenow is a plane tree grown mainly as an ornamental in the USA and Western Europe, and a significant source of airborne allergens in cities.

# FIVE QUATRAINS

*Points of view*
A pheasant green and gold beneath the skies
Brings tears of joy to contemplative eyes;
To others, opposite as north from south,
It merely brings a watering of the mouth.

*Verdict*
How blue the corn-flowers gleam amid the corn;
Upon a cloth of gold, contrasting beads.
The farmer looks and turns away with scorn;
    His only comment: "Weeds!"

*Diatoms seen under the microscope*[62]
On this glass slip, one inch by three,
A world of star-like beauty lies –
In microscopic rivalry
With mightier stars across the skies.

*The lonely fir-tree*
A fir, by stray breeze seeded, stands alone
Amid the brackens of the lowland plain;
And to the distant hills its sighing boughs
    Are ever stretched in vain.

*Cloud-shadows*
We are like children playing in an attic:
We know so little of the world around,
That it is self-defeat to be dogmatic
About the odds and ends that we have found.

---

[62] A diatom (from the Greek *dia* = through and *temnein* = to cut) is one of the most common types of phytoplankton, of which there are more than 200 *genera*; most live in open water; they are usually microscopic, although some species can reach up to two millimetres in length.

# SONG OF ONCOMING SPRING[63]

Dead the days of Winter anguish,
Spring and Life return to reign,
Laughter that so long did languish
Hovers round the lips again.
Eyes forlorn, once sealed with weeping,
Open to the sun anew;
And the tears from eyelids seeping
Flash their joy like springtime dew.
Swift-dissolving clouds of thunder
Now reveal the skies' blue wonder.

Night is vanquished and the morrow
Glimmers on the brightening slope;
Black, the bitter shade of sorrow,
Turns to golden fire of hope.
Drifted snows, by Winter fashioned,
Melt upon the springtime grass,
And the soaring Soul impassioned
Laughs to see them shrink and pass;
Laughs with Love of Spring begotten,
Laughs till Winter is forgotten.

Seeds that in the earth were buried
Burst a path towards the sky,
And their flowers' scent is ferried
On the breeze that eddies by.
Birds return across the billow
Where they fled from Winter's might;
Every aspen, oak and willow
Holds a choir of shrill delight,

---

[63] This, and the following poem, 'Egocentrism', are extracts from Stephanides' unpublished tragedy *The Bridge of Arta*, derived from a well-known folk-song of the same name, describing human sacrifice as a prerequisite for the successful building of the bridge. Versions of the folk-song exist throughout the Greek-speaking world.

Songs that over hill and hollow
Blend with skirl of homing swallow.

Sing then! Echo Maytime praises,
Voice the wingèd fleet,
Lightly brush the dancing daisies
With a ring of dancing feet.
Sing and dance! This moment matters;
All else is unborn or past;
Soon the rose is blown to tatters
By returning Winter blast.
But this day knows only gladness
And the swirl of Life's sweet madness!

Dance then! Brush the swaying grasses
With a ring of footsteps light;
Whisper not that Springtime passes,
Scorn the waiting Winter night!
Sing and dance, the dark unheeding,
Thrill the sunlit hours away,
Love and Laughter ever leading
Through the fragrant fields of May!
Follow after! Follow, frenzied!
Spring and Life together blended!

EGOCENTRISM

To life I seem so closely bound
The world seems one with me,
I feel the sun could not swing round
If I should cease to be.
I cannot picture in my brain,
I cannot realise
That Spring will bloom as fair again
Though seen through other eyes.

## PAUPER'S BURIAL

We greet the coffin and its burden mute
Head reverently bared or with salute...
Why do we honour thus the unknown dead
To whom, when living, none did honour give?

— You honour, mortal, one who has now read
The riddle *you* can never solve... and live!


## PALINODE (Song)

The tunes we heard when dreaming
We hear, awake, once more
Deep in the windy forest
Or by the rocky shore.
For the leaf that sighs or rustles
And the wave that rolls and gleams,
Recall with their own music
The music of our dreams.

The tunes we heard when roaming
Along the rocky shore
Or in the windy forest
Shall gladden us once more.
For the leaf that sighs and rustles
And the wave that rolls and gleams,
Create with their own music
The music of our dreams.

## TWO SEAGULLS (Oxford, March 1958)

I saw a pair of seagulls far inland…
Amid a new-ploughed field, they seemed to be
Two flakes of foam flung from the distant sea
On russet loam instead of golden sand.

And, as I watched and saw them drift and rise
Like flakes of foam borne on the ocean wind,
From days long past I visioned in my mind
Love-haunted shores beneath Ionian skies.

# FIVE QUATRAINS

*Impossible task*
In drifts of brown and yellow floating by,
The leaves of autumn flutter from the sky;
But vainly would you seek to count them all –
The leaves of Autumn *never* cease to fall...

*Death*
You shun my face, yet for my sister, Sleep,
You ever call to staunch the tears you weep.
You slumber but to wake and weep once more,
While those *I* kiss sleep sound for evermore.

*Prayer*
When I was young, I thought that life was meant
For happiness – my *hubris* I repent.
O foresworn Life, I ask no more for joy;
Spare me the sorrow and I'll be content.

*Atlantis*
A questing moon shone on an empty sea...
Only a drifting corpse, a floating tree,
Still marked the passing of a once famed shore
Whose hills would greet a rising sun no more.

*Magnets*
The compass-needle courts the pole
Across far leagues of land and sea;
My heart, too, seeks your own for goal
    With parallel fidelity.

## DEAD LEAVES

Dead leaves to the earth are sleeting
As the Autumn twilight fades,
Each an echoed sigh repeating
Twittering songs in springtime glades.

Dead leaves on my heart are falling
As Life's Autumn twilight wanes,
Each a memory recalling
Whispered words in springtime lanes.

## ONCOMING ELD

Sometimes I pause, and suddenly my mind
Becomes a blank and I just sit there still,
Quite still and motionless and yet not blind –
Simply indifferent and void of will.
Content to sit and watch, without a frown,
The Clock of Life serenely running down.

RED UPAS
(*This poem appeared in* Truth *magazine on 15 May 1953*)

The shadow of the Upas Tree lies dark
Across the world; its roots disrupt and blight
Earth's inmost core; its branches dim the light
Of Beauty and of laughing Joy; the spark
Of Reason, Man's Promethean attribute,
Is chilled and stifled by its poison-haze.

The soul's ecstatic Muses cower mute,
And the proud Centaurs of the spirit gaze
Afar off, wondering, at this Thing that Man,
Renouncing his past promise of the skies,
Now bows to crying: "Hail, O Upas Tree!
Hail, hail, O mighty Upas! We, who ban
The Star-God from His Own bright galaxies,
Have stopped our eyes with dust to worship thee!"


QUERY
(*This poem appeared in* Truth *magazine on 22 May 1953*)

"Brawn before Brains!" is now the parrot cry;
It is the fashion to extol the 'Worker'
And damn his brainier brother for a shirker.
But then, according to this logic, why
Does not the carter hand his horse the reins?
It has more brawn… and even fewer brains.

## THE PERFECT DEMAGOGUE

He has the rabble-rousing voice,
The boorish pertinacity,
The mean-souled grudge against the world,
The unashamed mendacity.
He has the egoist's conceit,
The fatuous imbecility,
The asinine intolerance,
The irresponsibility.
He has the jutting jaw and scowl
To overawe spectators,
He has, in short, the choicest traits
Of all the best dictators.


## ORATOR

When you run out of arguments
And all your quibbles fail,
Then drag a good red-herring
Across the wordy trail.
Just shunt the whole discussion
Onto another track,
And floor your dazed opponent
With voluble attack.
Shout, bray your very loudest,
Let only *you* be heard,
Your deafened audience will then think
That *you* had the last word!

# FIVE QUATRAINS

*Corcyra*[64]
Some who have known a well-loved site
Are chained for ever by its might;
Though they may wander as they will,
Remembered landscapes haunt them still.

*Nostalgia for the past*
The day is fading round me with the light,
The darkening shadows close upon their prey;
But, shining ever brighter through the night,
I see reflected gleams of yesterday.

*Cyprus 1974…*
We stood by Britain in her wars
And followed where she gave the lead;
She used us when the need was *hers*,
But failed us in *our* hour of need![65]

*After the blow-up*
Said Star-men, picking up the pieces:
"Man's henceforth an *endangered species*.
The few stray Humans we can find,
We must protect from their own kind."

*Dirge (after a Greek folk-song)*
We buried you, my darling one,
My heart's own love and light;
And with the radiance of your sun
The World of Shades grew bright.

---

[64] Corcyra is one of the ancient names for the island of Corfu (Kerkyra).
[65] Cyprus holds an ambivalent place in British foreign policy. In the 1950s the EOKA movement, which advocated *enosis* (union) with Greece, caused a political crisis which Britain was unable to resolve. Britain, Greece and Turkey agreed to its independence in 1960, but, following a Greek-instigated coup in 1974, the northern part of Cyprus was occupied by Turkish forces, and to this day the island remains divided.

## NO HERO

The Heron said: "A hero I would be,
If I could throw my useless 'n' away!"
But Mrs. Heron overheard, and she
Had quite a lot to say.

Born in the Zoo of London Town, she missed
The subtle point of her smart husband's pun:
"So I'm a useless 'en, am I?" she hissed,
"Take that and that, you fat conceited 'un!"

She pecked him good and hard and turned him out,
This lesson firmly planted in his brain:
"When my dear wife is anywhere about,
I must not pun again".

## HISTORIAN'S HEADACHE

A day at last will come (for aeons pass),
When to a question from his History-class:
"Was Alexander, Lord of Tunis, son
Or father of Philip of Macedon?",
The teacher, hesitating, will reply:
"I'll look it up and tell you by-and-by".[66]

---

[66] Philip of Macedon was father of Alexander the Great, the leader of the Hellenic world in the fourth century BC. Harold Alexander (1891–1969) was a military figure in the Second World War, created Earl Alexander of Tunis in recognition of his role as Commander-in-Chief of the Mediterranean forces.

## MY FAIR-HAIRED DARLING
*(from the original Greek poem by Dionysios Solomos, 1798–1859)*[67]

I saw my fair-haired darling,
I saw her yesterday,
I saw her in the twilight
Before she sailed away.

A breeze blew ever stronger
To fill each snow-white sail;
The ship was like a sea-gull
That glides upon the gale.

And we who had so loved her
Looked out across the sea...
The farewell scarf she fluttered
Seemed meant alone for me.

The farewell scarf she fluttered
Held both my heart and gaze,
Until with gathering darkness
I lost it in the haze.

For just a few more moments
I thought I saw it loom –
Was it the scarf that glimmered,
Or a foam-flake in the gloom?

At last the ship's white top-sail
Slid softly from our sight;
But we who had so loved her
Still searched the empty night.

---

[67] This is a loose translation of verses 1–6 of Solomos' 'I Xanthoula' ['The Fair-haired Girl'] from *Apanda* (*Collected Works*) vol. I, ed. Linos Politis (Athens: Ikaros, 1986) pp. 65–6.

## EPITAPH TO THE ISLAND OF PSARA
*(from the original Greek poem by Dionysios Solomos)*[68]

On Psara, amid smoke eddies streaming,
Glory paces alone in her dreaming,
And she broods o'er the dead as she passes,
And she carries a wreath in her hand –
A wreath of a few withered grasses
That had clung to that desolate land.


## FLOWERS

The woodland flowers greet the day
And feel no need for praise;
Their clusters crowd along the way
In colourful arrays,
That seek no eyes to watch them grow
And joy in their prismatic glow.

But other flowers greet the skies
And, of less hardy race,
They crave the warmth of gazing eyes,
The love in voice and face –
If left too long in lonely glade,
Their petals droop, they wilt, they fade…

---

[68] The small rugged island of Psara, near Chios in the Aegean sea, was the site of resistance by the islanders during the war of independence from the Ottoman empire: many islanders killed themselves with explosives under the banner 'Freedom or Death' on 4 July 1821, inspiring Dionysios Solomos to compose his epigram 'I Katastrofi ton Psaron' ['The Destruction of Psara'] in *Apanda* vol. I, p. 139. Stephanides reproduces the anapaestic structure of Solomos' poem.

## THE HAUNTED TARN

Sighing reeds and moaning rushes
Sway. The wind that wails and hushes
Stirs the lakelet darkly gleaming
Where a pale mist, upward streaming,
Dims the moonbeams' light.

And a pale ghost skyward gazes,
To each star her arms she raises;
But the heavens, never caring,
Unrelenting roll, unsparing,
Till she sinks from sight.

Then, from out the water peering,
Looms a visage dark and sneering;
And a screech of cruel laughter,
With the echoes jeering after,
Screams across the night!

## ROSES (*after a Greek folk-song*)

How sad the rose that on her breast once lay
Should now be scentless, withered, brown and dry;
While other roses, flowering on her tomb,
Should flaunt their freshness in the joy of day
And, quivering to the kiss of sun and sky,
Should greet the springtime breeze with sweet perfume!

# FIVE QUATRAINS

*Predicament*
Love carelessly discharged a dart
That, curving back, pierced his own heart…
What should he do, this archer daft,
Thus wounded by his own keen shaft?

*The torch*
The Flame devours the torch from which it gains
    Its blazing light;
And Love, too, sears the heart till there remains
    But ash in the cold night.

*Convivial love*
With Bacchus Eros loves to sup,
All night he empties cup on cup;
Still drunk, his arrows he dispatches —
And brings off some hilarious matches!

*Paradox*
The amethyst is said to be
For drunkenness a remedy;
But when it glances from your eyes
Intoxication in it lies!

*Love's tempest*
I thought to sail upon the blue
Of Love's calm reaches in your eyes;
But they reflect a stormier hue
And lightning flashes from their skies!

THE PYRE (*after a Greek folk-song*)

When I am dead, in a forest glade
My bones will slumber the winter through;
But a smouldering glow will never fade
From my dream-filled breast for love of you.
A tiny gleam will awake with spring
Till a spark is born from my heart's pent fire,
And a scorching flame with its crimson wing
Shall fan the trees for my funeral pyre!


INQUEST

Each night it was Leander's wont
Across the stormy Hellespont
To gain his darling's side.
But in the end it finished him –
Was it the maiden or the swim?...
We only know he died.

Yet still Leanders can be found
All set in icy deeps to bound
Just for a sweetheart's sake.
To such we cry: "Don't lose your head;
'Twas *figurative* when she said
'Go jump into a lake!'"

# TREE OF REMEMBRANCE

I shun the tree we loved in days gone by
Lest I should hear, when listening in its shade
To your sweet whisper that can never fade,
The sound of other kiss and other sigh.
I shun that tree for, when Decembers loom,
Its branches, dead and black against the sky,
Seem fleshless fingers pointing through the gloom
Towards a spot where amaranths yet lie.
I shun that tree for, after winter gaunt
Has been outpaced by April's eager wings,
Its branches, foaming into blossom, taunt
Me with their new-found life that mates and sings.

The tree we loved! I shun it, yet I find
That round my heart its every root is twined.


# EXONERATION

She bit into the apple,
Its flesh was crisp and white;
She bit into the apple –
And blood gushed from the bite!
She paused a startled moment,
Then tossed a careless head;
The apple's flesh was tasty,
What matter that it bled.

SONG

Over the mountains
The swallow is seen,
Winging by fountains
Where willows are green,
Winging by waters
Where willows are green.

But a lone heart bides sleeping
In winter's dark night,
A-wearied from weeping
For springtime and light,
A-wearied from waiting
For Love and for Light.


THRENODY

How sad that they who once were dear to me
Should seem to grow more shadowy and remote
With every ebbing year. Their faces fade
Although my memory tries hard to hold
Their evanescent features in its grasp.
Remembered eyes that once I knew so bright
Have lost their former clearness as if Time
Had dulled my own eyes with a dimming veil.
Remembered voices whisper far away
And grow more faint; the slowly passing years
Have raised a wall that muffles every sound
Till even its own echo seems unreal.

Is it old-age that makes the heart less fond,
Or is the brain the culprit? Why should I,
Now loitering before an Opening Gate,
Feel, somehow, as though I had failed the Dead?...

# DELAYED JOURNEY

I looked out of my window
While the sky was yet at night,
And I saw the moonlight shining
Upon a wintry plain.
And I wondered if the sun had died,
And if this frozen light
Was but its ghost returning
To haunt the world again.

Then, from the railway station,
I heard a wailing scream,
And a many-jointed serpent
Rushed by in fiery spate.
"A flaming dragon passeth!"
I cried. To which my dream
Tee-heed: "And thus thou missest
The seven twenty-eight!"

# FIVE QUATRAINS

*Wasted arrow*
Love laid an ambush for us two,
His arrow pierced me through and through;
But alas! upon *your* heart
Its barb in splinters flew apart.

*Radiance*
As he who gazes at the sun
Is dazzled by the skies,
So he who looks upon your face
Sees everywhere your eyes!

*Entreaty*
My love, a jewelled gift I bring,
And with it I would linger;
Oh, twist and wear me like this ring
Around your little finger!

*Reproach*
Your eyes are like the looking-glass
That in your hand you hold:
Though they reflect my face, alas!
They still stay mirror-cold.

*Love's Icarus*
You granted me the wings of Love
And I flew to the light;
But, plumed with golden lies, those wings
Could not sustain my flight.

# GHOSTLY BALLAD

When the evening sun has set,
Ocean-borne, the silhouette
Of an island reaches high,
Stabbing lance-like at the sky.
And the clouds' candescent blood
Stains the wave tops in a flood
Of reflected crimson light.
Onward sweeps relentless night
Till day's lingering colours, banished,
Slowly, one by one, have vanished;
And a gloom succeeds their mirth
Over sea and sky and earth...

Then upon a darkened cape
Softly glides a vaporous shape,
And a maiden fair to see
Stands in lonely misery.
Pale she is as autumn mist
By the rising sun unkissed,
And her limbs transparent gleam
As the flow of mountain stream.
To the sea's encroaching tide
Turns she with her arms flung wide,
And her distant voice is heard
Like the cry of ocean bird:

"Loved one, many a weary year
Did I stand in faith or fear
On the brow of yonder cliff,
Waiting for your homing skiff.
Often, gazing through the gale,
Foam-flakes took I for your sail,
But, like foam upon the wave,
Died my wasted hopes. My grave
Loomed at last, a headstone white,

On that seaward-jutting height
Whence for all those endless years
I had sought you through my tears.
There upon that cliff I lay,
Lingering night and livelong day,
While the west-wind and the sea
Whispered of eternity…

"Yestereve a storm arose
And, amid its frenzied throes,
Breakers lashed with fiercer roar
At their age-old foe, the shore.
Quaked the cliff with every blow,
Quaked the overhanging brow,
Till along a widening rift
Its whole margin, torn adrift,
Crashed below into the wave,
Bearing in its fall my grave.
Now upon this wave-worn beach
Which the deep-sea billows reach,
Have my bleaching bones been cast –
Loved one, come to me at last!"

Far away across the main
Soars a gleam to sink again,
Borne amid the breakers' roar
Ever nearer to the shore.
Ever closer looms that light,
Brightening against the night,
And a distant voice is heard
Like the cry of ocean bird:

"Loved one, on the wind-whipped tide
Sped my skiff to gain your side;
But upon a treacherous reef
Came my fragile barque to grief.
Deep down deep beneath the foam,

All my thoughts to you did home,
But I could not leave the wave
Hemming me in deep-sea grave.
There beneath the tide I lay,
Lingering night and livelong day,
While the west-wind and the sea
Whispered of eternity...

"Ever were my dreams of you:
Wondering if your love was true;
Or if, lip to lip, your breast
Other fingers had caressed.
Ah, how often grew the brine
Bitterer yet with tears of mine,
Welling from my sockets blind
When such visions held my mind!
Year by year, the sand-banks shifted,
Deep-sea currents churned and drifted,
And my hollow bones they bore
Ever nearer to the shore.

"Yestereve a storm arose
And, amid its frenzied throes,
Quaked the very seas with dread
To their dark abysmal bed.
Undertows, amid the shades,
Rasped along the ocean glades,
Raising clouds of inky slime
Dormant since the birth of time,
Hustling in their shoreward sweep
Torpid monsters of the deep,
Crushing corallines and shells
And Medusa's crystal bells!

"Mingled with the weeds and stones,
Eddies swirled around my bones,
And the ocean's mighty hand

Urged them on towards the land.
Ah, beloved, it is the day
When our souls shall meet for aye,
When for us relenting Fate
Opens wide a long closed Gate.
Loved one, see, upon the shingle
Now our bones together mingle,
For at last the cruel main
Reunites us both again!"

   \* \* \*

On a slanting surge reclining,
Two clasped forms are seen entwining,
And the breaker lifts them high
As it towers to the sky.
Then two star-flakes, silvery-white,
Glide together through the night,
Till they seem to blend afar –
Brighter than the Evening Star.

# THE TALE OF PRUE, THE PRUDENT VAMPIRE
*(Written in hospital, after having my umpteenth 'blood specimen' taken. October 1972)*

A beautiful vampire arose from the dead;
Her hair was jet black and her lips ruby red,
Her skin was snow-white and her eyes were sea-green,
The sweetest young vampire that ever was seen.

She would have been perfect, for nothing she lacked,
Except for the rather unfortunate fact
That she was a *vampire*, and consequently she
Was not quite the girl-friend for you or for me.

She arose from her grave (as I mentioned before)
And her very first thought was for gallons of gore,
But her name it was 'Prudence' and prudent she was
And wily and wary and watchful, because

She knew that the public had been saturated
With horror-films showing how ghouls are check-mated.
Fresh blood! How to get it – ah, there was the riddle,
Without a big stake being shoved through your middle.

Prue pondered and pondered. "My name will be mud",
Said she, "if I cannot get buckets of blood;
But how do it safely?" She thought for a while,
Then shouted "Eureka!" and smiled a sly smile.

Now in every big hospital in London you'll meet
A busy young Sister, white-aproned and neat.
She pushes a trolley, by day and by night,
With test-tubes and bottles all shining and bright.

She comes to your bed and, with sweetness and charm,
She sticks a sharp needle right into your arm

And fills a whole syringe with your vintage gore,
And then does the same to the patient next door.

It is she! It is Prudence! She knows very well
That in a big hospital no one can tell
What *anyone's* doing; and so you can bet
That Prue and her trolley have not been stopped yet.

She punctures the patients without stint or stay;
Unhindered, she visits the wards every day;
She fills all her bottles with blood fresh and hot –
Then she slinks round a corner and guzzles the lot!

# THE TEMPEST
*or, the unfortunate influence of motoring on the muse*

'Mid the whirlwind's seething welter
Strove a goodly ship and true
To attain a haven's shelter
O'er the abyss of the blue.
Lashed she was by angry billows
Spouted from the seething main,
And her masts were bent like willows
And her bridge was rent in twain.
And the spindrift dripped in runnels
From each thrumming spar and stay,
And the smoke belched from her funnels
As she ploughed her stubborn way.

(*Inspiration short-circuited by friend with two-seater. Interval devoted to m.p.h. and liquid refreshment. Poem resumed on return.*)

For his ship the skipper battled,
Warring with the ocean swell,
And he never once got rattled
For he knew his duty well.
"Man the gears!" his voice resounded,
"And the starboard clutch downhaul!"
As one man the whole crew bounded
While the ship leant from the squall.
The chief-engineer came reeling,
Pale and grim amid the rout,
"All is lost!" he shrieked with feeling,
"For the off hind screw's blown out!"
But the skipper did not falter
As he cried "Then fix the spare".
And his course he did not alter
And he did not turn a hair.
Firm he stood amid the flaring
Of the lightning-riven dark

When the first-mate wailed, despairing,
That the compass would not spark;
When the fog obscured the tideways
And the brakes had come to grief,
And the ship was skidding sideways
On the fatal Barrier Reef!
But the skipper without bustle,
Brows knit in a steady frown,
Calmly ordered "Now, lads, hustle!
Let the shock-absorbers down".
Thus he foiled the rocky splinters
Poised to pierce his vessel through,
Shoals that had for countless winters
Taken toll of craft and crew.
Aye, the ship, with scarce a shudder,
Of those hungry fangs made sport;
And the skipper seized the rudder
And garaged her safe in port.

# FIVE QUATRAINS

*Sport up to date*
The rhino charged with tail in air,
I did not even turn a hair.
I aimed my good bazooka – whump!
And blew his snout right through his rump.

*"When soft voices die" (with apologies to Percy B. Shelley)*[69]
Voices, whether harsh or clear,
Must die at last upon the ear.
Some singers too, had I the choice,
Would die together with the voice.

*The hypochondriac's epitaph (after the ancient Greek)*
See! I was right in spite of all their jeers,
I who this grave now fill:
I kept on telling them for eighty years
That I was *really* ill.

*Divergence*
With bonnets some would guard their brains
From sunstroke, chills and suchlike strains;
But others use them, if you please,
As perambulating apiaries.

*Remedy*
The times were out of joint he thought,
    So overnight.
He wrote a letter to *The Times*
    And put them right.

---

[69] Shelley wrote 'Music, when soft voices die, / Vibrates in the memory – / Odours, when sweet violets sicken, / Live within the sense they quicken. / Rose leaves, when the rose is dead, / Are heap'd for the beloved's bed; / And so thy thoughts, when thou art gone, / Love itself shall slumber on.'

# THE WRECK OF THE SCHOONER *HESPERUS*[70]
(as remembered from childhood)

It was the Schooner Hesperus
That sailed the wintry sea,
And the skipper had taken his little daughter
To keep him company.

"Oh skipper, reef the mizzen-mast"
Cried the bosun from below,
"For I hear the breakers roaring loud
On the Reef of Norman's Woe!"

But the skipper answered never a word,
Whilst all the planks did shrink;
There was water, water everywhere,
But not a drop to drink!

The bosun stood on the burning deck
Whence all but he had fled,
Till the skipper's daughter took his hand
And tearfully she said:

"Tom Bowling lies a sheer, sheer hulk,
The darling of the fleet,

---

[70] TS was having great and irresponsible fun constructing this poem, with parodical echoes of Longfellow's original poem *The Wreck of the Hesperus* and its reference to the reef of Norman's Woe near Boston, but also of poems by Felicia Dorothea Hemans ('Casabianca': 'The boy stood on the burning deck'), Coleridge ('The Rime of the Ancient Mariner': 'Water, water, everywhere. / Nor any drop to drink') and Lesley Nelson-Burns ('Tom Bowling': 'Here a sheer hulk lies poor Tom Bowling. / The darling of our crew'). Richard Kempenfelt (1718–82) was a British admiral whose boat, *The Royal George*, sank with loss of approximately 900 lives when it became overloaded with a cargo of rum.

But my heart was lost with Kempenfelt
And all his crew complete!"

Then the skipper paced the binnacle
And his face was wan with woe,
For he had shot the albatross
That made the winds to blow;

And now the Schooner *Hesperus*
Was drifting with the swell,
And the skipper tore his white, white hair,
For he heard the Inchcape Bell.

A land breeze shook the Schooner's shrouds
And she was overset,
Down went the Schooner *Hesperus* –
And she is down there yet!

## NOT SO *PIANO*

The music poured out of the piano
As her fingers belaboured the keys,
The notes tumbled over each other
Like the breakers of turbulent seas.

The notes tumbled over each other
Like waves on a storm-battered shore:
Base notes and grace notes
And high notes and wry notes,
While the guests cried politely "Encore!"

She played and she still went on playing
Although it was long after nine,
The notes tumbled over each other
And bumped up and down every spine.

The notes tumbled over each other
Like a thunder-cloud's echoing roar:
Grace, base and high notes
And billions of wry notes,
Till the guests moaned forlornly "No more!"


## MY LOVE CAME TRIPPING, TRIPPING…

My love came tripping, tripping,
The sweetest flower that blows,
Her eyes the hue of violets,
Her cheeks the blush of rose.
My love came tripping, tripping,
She swayed as hare-bells sway,
And said: "Oh blast this hearth-rug,
It'll break my neck some day!"

# EIGHT DISTICHS

*Revolt*
Said one Parallel Line to another: "My sweet,
Let's cause consternation – in short, let us meet!"

*Distraction*
A cuckoo once said to his mate: "I'll be blessed!
I'm so absent-minded, I've built you a nest".

*Politician*
"No one can stop me! *I'll* show them, by heck!"
But he stopped right enough when he met with a cheque.

*Immoral tale*
A tradesman who betted on horses for fun,
Went broke and went to the dogs – and won!

*Relativity*
Relativity conscious, a tortoise did cry:
"That car's standing still, and it's me whizzing by!"

*Nature note*
Said the moth: "You a firefly? You must be unhinged!
I flew round you all night and I'm not even singed".

*Verdict*
The Crown of Virtue there are some who win,
Who never were alive enough to sin.

*Moth*
I am the moth that wheels in fluttering rings,
Your glance the flame in which I scorch my wings!

COMPLAINT

The Muse decrees that epigrams
Should be concise and witty,
But when I seek her patronage
She fools me without pity.
She makes me burn my midnight oil
(Or rather electricity),
And then she leaves me in the lurch
With maddening duplicity!


BAD CURRENCY

Bad currency drives out the good –
A law known but too well:
The cuckoo kills the linnet chick
Ere it can leave its shell.
And likewise does the Bastard Muse
Of 'Modern Verse' displace
The Pierian Muse who shrinks in fear
From her distorted face.

## AFTER MANY YEARS

I saw the Fir I planted long ago
When I was young and it was but a seed;
And I remembered how I watched it grow,
Protecting, shielding it from blight and weed.

Then, as I gazed, Time backwards seemed to flow:
The Fir a seedling and I young again...
And I remembered how I watched it grow,
And all the Past awakened in my brain.

The Fir's tall crest above me to and fro
Waved in the wind, I saw it toss and sway;
And I remembered how I watched it grow —
But it sighed for the mountains far away.

## ULTIMATE GOAL

Should happiness be Man's controlling aim?
Some who now lead him preach for only goal
Materialistic futures; whilst the soul
Is dispossessed, and thwarted of all claim
To actuality. Man's questing mind
They seek to cramp in mould of dull content.
To such drab guides the Road of Humankind
Is not towards the stars, but a descent,
By pleasant paths, into some valley deep
Where lush green grass is best enjoyed by sheep.

## 80ᵀᴴ BIRTHDAY (21–I–1976)

It seems quite *comic* that I should be old!
How vivid is the spell of those far days
When all the world sang to a sun of gold;
And heart and mind, blent in its golden blaze,
Were freed to gladness by a golden thrill
That lingers even yet! Far days they seem
When the past reckoning of every chill,
Dead, buried sun is tallied gleam by gleam.

But days are fleeting gauged in hopes and fears,
Mere moments that have ebbed with silent speed –
Is *this* the only harvest of their seed:
This little life with all its thwarted years?
For, as I wait amid the gathering night,
Remembered dawns reflect the only light…


## EVENING DOUBTS (1978)

There was a dawn when verses, metres, rhymes,
Came singing through my brain. Difficulty
Was in the choice and, so it seemed to me,
The winnowing of white from black. At times
I wonder now how often I was wrong,
If what I took for white was only grey;
If I retained the doggerel, not the song,
And threw the Muses' whisperings away.

Or did my ears mislead me? Were the notes
I thought were sung by woodland nightingales,
But awkward parodies, discordant scales
Squawked mockingly from crows' ironic throats?

Could I choose better as night falls?… But how? –
I hear no more those singing voices now…

# FIVE QUATRAINS

*Epitaph to a politician*
Here lies the only Party Man
Who died by all respected.
(He choked upon a herring bone
The day he was elected.)

*Poet's predicament*
It's maddening that there should be
One rhyme alone for 'Cupid';
A rhyme the poet cannot use,
Because it's simply... stupid!

*The modern poet*
He fashions gems of exquisite design
With a technique no craftsman could surpass;
And then, instead of mounting them in gold,
    He uses brass.

*Endeavour*
The mountaineer toiled upwards
With many a gasp and pant;
The mountain was a mole-hill –
But the climber was an ant!

*The Parthenon*
I scorn the buffetings of War and Time.
The centuries have ever crowned me Queen,
And pilgrims gather yet from every clime
Fair gems among my shattered stones to glean.

# Bishop's Move

## Bishop's Move

Lawrence Durrell was a man of striking appearance whose aristocratic features and high-domed forehead made him conspicuous in any crowd. His impressive, clean-shaven face would often take on a benign expression; this was most noticeable after meals as Durrell, like all geniuses, was particularly fond of the good things of life. His post-prandial countenance was, at times, so saintly that it was often likened to that of a churchman of high degree.

As the years went by, Durrell got to be taken more and more frequently for a bishop; and this, undoubtedly, influenced his character. His deportment grew more ecclesiastic and his frequent expletives took on an episcopal flavour, such as "Dash my gaiters!" or "Blow my baldachin!" He would also, quite unconsciously, raise his right hand aloft and, if the said hand did not hold a filled glass, his fingers would join in the recognised gesture of benediction.

This happened one fine afternoon just as a certain Mr. Patrick Murphy was leaving the *Toad and Gosling* at the urgent request of a muscular barman. Mr. Murphy, much elevated by this apparent episcopal blessing, reeled round the corner and assaulted a passing traction engine. The latter emerged victorious from this fracas, and, a few minutes later, Mr. Murphy found himself confronting Saint Peter at the Pearly Gates.

"Well, Mr. Patrick Murphy," said Saint Peter, who of course knew everybody, "I think you've come to the wrong address. Take the next down-escalator; it will deliver you to where you rightly belong. Goodbye!"

"I believe that you are mistaken, Sir" replied Patrick Murphy, whose grammar and diction had benefited considerably from his sudden transition. "I died within the statutory three-hour limit after having received an episcopal benediction, and I accordingly passed over in a State of Grace. Plenary remission of all sins included."

Saint Peter looked up, startled. But it did not even occur to him to doubt Murphy's statement. It was too well known that nobody, not even Ananias himself, could possibly utter a falsehood within the precincts of the Golden City. "You were lucky," he growled, "very, very lucky indeed. But your legal rights cannot be contested. So pass, friend, and all's well!"

An hour later, a distraught heavenly Being stood before Saint Peter. "Angel Ezekiah, Sir," he announced, "from the Recording Department. I have come to report a terrible error concerning one of my assignees, a certain Patrick Alistair Murphy. I have just seen him disporting himself on the Nursery Clouds, practising aerial telemarks on his wings, and twanging a harp Mark IV B. He was let in without my being consulted, and despite the fact that he was booked for the Other Place. See, I can prove it from my records!"

"There, there, now," said Saint Peter soothingly, "calm yourself; everything is under control. Mr. Murphy died within three hours of an episcopal blessing. He has, consequently, a legal right to be here. Sins cancelled – all shipshape and correct."

"But that's exactly where you're wrong, Sir!" screamed the Angel excitedly. "Patrick Murphy was not blessed by a bishop. He was blessed by a certain Mr. Lawrence Durrell, a person of no official status – not even a lay-preacher or other accredited amateur!"

"Come, come, my good Angel, you are letting your prejudices run away with you!" exclaimed Saint Peter testily. "Of course Murphy was blessed by a bishop! He said so *himself*. And, as you well know, nobody can possibly lie *here*."

"That's just the trouble, Sir," wailed the Angel. "Murphy *wasn't* lying – he honestly believed that he *had* been blessed by a bishop. But that doesn't make it that he *was*. And now you've let him in, Sir, and what can we do about it?"

There was a stunned silence. At last Saint Peter enquired ominously, "Do you mean to tell me that Mr. Lawrence Durrell dared to commit the unpardonable crime of impersonating a bishop!? What were the Archangels with their fiery swords doing? There must have been a gross dereliction of duty somewhere!"

"No, Sir" quavered the Angel unhappily. "The Archangels couldn't do a thing. Mr. Durrell was not impersonating a bishop; he was simply *looking like* a bishop. It is not yet an indictable offence to *look like* a bishop. And in the meanwhile, Sir, what are we to do about Mr. Patrick Murphy? We can't boot him out without admitting that we let him in by mistake."

"Heaven makes NO mistakes!" said Saint Peter stiffly. "If we started admitting mistakes, everybody in the Other Establishment would be clamouring about miscarriages of justice – Lucifer himself might demand a retrial! No, we must think of some other way... Ha! I have just the right solution. Since all this trouble started because Mr. Lawrence Durrell was not a real bishop, the only way is to *make* him a real bishop. With seniority back-dated five minutes before Mr. Murphy received his benediction. *That* should make everything perfectly legal. And a minor miracle of this sort is well within the capacity of one of the junior Archangels – we won't need to drag in the top brass. So run along, my good Ezekiah, and see that my order is carried out with the utmost forthwithness."

\* \* \*

Lawrence Durrell left the portals of the *Jamshid Restaurant* feeling at peace with the world. That prawn curry had been really excellent, and those two bottles of *Chateauneuf-Lapompe* superlative! As he sauntered along, he sensed a slight constriction around his calves; he noticed also that several women (one of them quite a luscious young blonde) had dropped him deep curtsies as he passed them by.

And who was this funny young man in a dog-collar who had been trotting along behind him for the last five minutes? Durrell turned on him with a good-natured smile. "What are you following me around for?" he enquired jocularly; "are you, perhaps, taking me for a bishop or something?"

The dog-collared one looked startled. "But you are a

bishop, your Grace!" he stuttered. "And, if I may be permitted to say so, one well up in the betting for the next vacant archbishopric."

A dazed expression played for a few seconds about Lawrence Durrell's mobile features. Then his face cleared. "Cor chase my chasubles," he assented, "so I am!"

www.ingramcontent.com/pod-product-compliance
Ingram Content Group UK Ltd.
Pitfield, Milton Keynes, MK11 3LW, UK
UKHW021813200226
468233UK00006B/26